658.82HEA

SUCCESSFUL SPONSORSHIP

VICTOR HEAD

Successful Sponsorship

PUBLISHED IN ASSOCIATION WITH
THE INSTITUTE OF DIRECTORS

DIRECTOR BOOKS

Published by Director Books,
Fitzwilliam Publishing Limited,
Simon & Schuster International Group,
Fitzwilliam House, 32 Trumpington Street,
Cambridge CB2 1QY, England

First published as *Sponsorship: the newest marketing skill*
in 1981 by Woodhead-Faulkner Ltd in association with
the Institute of Marketing.
Second edition 1988, published in association with the
Institute of Directors.

© Victor Head 1981, 1988

British Library Cataloguing in Publication Data

Head, Victor
Successful sponsorship.—2nd ed.
1. Great Britain. Sponsorship by business
firms—For marketing
I. Title
658.8'2

ISBN 1-870555-08-2

Designed by Geoff Green
Typeset by Quorn Selective Repro Ltd
Printed in Great Britain by A. Wheaton and Co. Ltd, Exeter

Contents

Preface

(TO THE SECOND EDITION)

Sponsorship in its modern guise as a form of company promotion, usually of sport or the arts, has come of age. Over the past two decades it has become an important factor in corporate communications and advertising which is shown by the fact that today in Britain business spends more than £200 million on sponsorship each year and more than half the major marketing companies have participated. Most of this money goes on sporting events which, by their nature, offer better opportunities for television and newspaper exposure, but the arts attract increasing support and the annual amount spent on them grew from £5 million to £30 million between 1981 and 1988. Such figures are only part of the story. Add the 'below-the-line' costs of publicity, marketing, entertaining, management, etc. that sponsors necessarily incur and the total figure can be doubled. Some authorities multiply the 'up-front' cost by a factor of three. We are, therefore, discussing a £400-million industry – more than ten per cent of the UK annual expenditure on television and press advertising.

All of this indicates fundamental changes in attitude. It does not mean that there has been a comparable increase in awareness of what sponsorship is and what it can and cannot achieve. Much has been written in newspapers, magazines and academic studies about sponsorship by observers intrigued by its rapid growth and diversity, but misconceptions still abound. This book, based on personal experience of sponsorship projects, may help to dispel these misconceptions and provide a compass for those about to set sail on this wide and largely unknown ocean.

After defining what is meant by sponsorship, the book traces its history and development, investigates financing and fund-raising, and deals comprehensively with the opportunities available in sport and the arts, before going on to offer guidance on identifying objectives, making a choice and servicing a selected project. Arts and sports organisations, and individuals, seeking sponsorship will, it is hoped, particularly appreciate the suggestions 'from the other side' on how to woo potential sponsors.

There is also advice for potential sponsors on how to spend their money most effectively by identifying reasonable expectations and making sure that their objectives are met, and numerous examples show how this has been done and how it has not. One aspect of the book that has proved particularly useful is a do-it-yourself chart (see page 109) for rapidly assessing a sponsorship's potential value. When this appeared in the first edition, it was the first time that anything like this had been devised. Since then, several companies and organisations both in the UK and overseas have reproduced this chart in their own publications.

April 1988   *V.H.*

Acknowledgements

I am very grateful for the help and advice given by a host of people and organisations, particularly the enthusiastic co-operation received from Luke Rittner, Secretary-General of the Arts Council and his predecessor, Sir Roy Shaw; Dickie Jeeps, then Chairman, and John Wheatley, Director-General of the Sports Council; Roger Underhill, Director-General of The Advertising Association; and Kenneth Miles, Director of the Incorporated Society of British Advertisers Ltd. Colin Tweedy, Director of the Association for Business Sponsorship of the Arts, and Edward M. Strauss, jr, President of the Business Committee for the Arts in New York, were most helpful, as indeed was the former Minister for the Arts, Norman St John-Stevas. The various sports authorities kindly made their archives available and much useful information was obtained by researchers Pat Parkin and Vicki Robinson.

V.H.

CHAPTER 1

Introduction and definition

The formidable lady in the sensible suit and no-nonsense spectacles was insistent. Through the hubbub of voices in the Crush Bar at the Royal Opera House, Covent Garden, her questions buzzed persistently like bluebottles at a window-pane. 'Well, how *do* you justify spending your company's money on the arts?' she demanded in the sort of tone that elderly waitresses use in some London clubs on members who haven't eaten all their rice pudding.

Once more I found myself adopting what Denis Norden calls his 'respectful, listening-to-opera face', and familiar phrases like 'social responsibility' and 'good corporate citizenship' came to mind. But before the argument could be developed into aspects of marketing, advertising, communications, public affairs, staff relations and all the other areas of business life upon which sponsorship has an impact, the bell summoned us to join Rodolfo at Mimi's deathbed and another opportunity was lost.

The lady was, in fact, a senior executive of one of Europe's largest industrial groups and she spent much of her time assessing appeals for financial aid from outside sources. She was benefactress to dozens of charities but her sceptical attitude towards sponsorship is not unknown, even today in Britain.

As I took my seat I recalled, with a sense of irony, a recent summer's evening in New York when something like 150,000 people picnicked and stargazed on the broad pasture of Sheep Meadows in Central Park and listened to the New York Philharmonic Orchestra playing Mahler and Beethoven. They did so by courtesy of Exxon which, at the same time, was financing a city street Latin music festival in the South Bronx at which all ages danced to the music of the Angel Canales y Orchestra playing on top of a gaudily decorated float. Also on that evening, the oil giant was extending a helping hand in Sitka, Alaska, to a chamber music concert, and away to the south in Houston's Hermann Park, the same corporate 'angel' was underwriting a performance of *Fiddler on the Roof*.

All this was part of its annual expenditure on arts and education of more than $5 million (in 1980). Exxon's support for the arts goes back certainly to 1944, when the company commissioned 16 American artists to create works that depicted oil's role in the war effort. In the following year Exxon money enabled Robert Flaherty to complete his classic documentary film *Louisiana Story*.

Of course, in the United States such corporate giving can be tax deductible, which might well be an inducement to would-be sponsors. There are other differences between Britain and America and I was somewhat surprised after addressing a conference in San Francisco on UK sponsorship to be told, 'You are light years ahead of us in this field'. Something of an overstatement, perhaps, in view of the history and diversity of sponsorship in America.

'The Prospect of a new Broadcasting Act has concentrated the corporate minds of the BBC and the IBA on reviewing their sponsorship policies. Privatisation of broadcasting in many European countries and the spread of satellite channels over the Continent have already paved the way for the kind of programme sponsorship long familiar to American, Australian and Japanese audiences', says Keith Yeomans, Director of Media Development and a former BBC producer.

Although in Britain commercial involvement in television programmes is at present limited to brief credits at the beginning and end plus the option of buying spots in the advertisement breaks, that is not the whole picture. As Yeomans stresses, television and radio can be used much more creatively. 'TV series can be created as showcases for products and services, with programmes at the sharp end of a sophisticated system of tie-in advertising, direct mailing and sales promotion – BBC's *Daytime Club* was a gesture in this direction.'

Such an idea will, understandably, arouse fears; people will want to know what the potential dangers of increased intervention in programmes might be. Clearly, strict supervision will be necessary, but Yeomans is optimistic: 'It is possible to safeguard standards while exploiting the commercial potential offered by media sponsorship'.

My own experiences in sponsorship, first as a journalist casting, at times, a jaundiced eye in its direction and, subsequently, as sponsorship organiser for a multinational insurance company, have convinced me of the importance of this subject about which so much is said and which is so little understood. In Britain business spends around £200 million a year on sponsorship and some authorities multiply this by up to three to take account of the hidden costs involved in making a sponsorship work.

As a marketing tool, it is still new, which makes it a particularly challenging and exciting area in which to work. The purpose of this book is to attempt, through a personal view of sponsorship over the past decade or so, to unravel some of its complexities for the benefit of both would-be sponsors and those who hope to be sponsored.

It is vital at the start of any sponsorship project, and certainly at the beginning of a book like this, to be absolutely clear what is meant by sponsorship. It is remarkable how often and where one encounters confusion. Ask any three executives with razor-sharp business minds to define what they mean by sponsorship and you will meet woolly thinking and contradictions. Government spokesmen, captains of industry and even many of those engaged in this growth activity will often disagree over definitions, and it is so easy to confuse sponsorship and patronage, or muddle charitable donations with the advertising budget.

Defining sponsorship is a bit like trying to harpoon a butterfly in a gale. As we know it today, it is something that has developed over the past 30 years, yet it has existed in some form for much longer than that. Even sports sponsorship is by no means a modern invention. The *News of the World*, for example, supported golf's match-play championship for 60 years. To sponsor, whether at the baptismal font or as a guarantor of surety in a contract, is noble. To help or support an enterprise, even if self-help is also involved, is no bad thing.

In the form of 'patronage' of the arts, sponsorship is centuries old. Dr Johnson may have given it a bad name with his famous letter to the niggardly Earl of Chesterfield in 1755 (see Chapter 2). But Dr Johnson did subsequently receive a government pension of £300 per annum, a form of state sponsorship.

In essence, modern sponsorship is a mutually beneficial business arrangement between sponsor and sponsored to achieve defined objectives. This, of course, could also apply to other things, but it helps us to separate it from what is more obviously simple advertising.

As an illustration of some of the possible complications, take the case of a firm that agrees to support a charitable enterprise, not with cash, but by paying for an advertisement in, say, a gala concert programme. Is it a charitable donation, a form of sponsorship or does it come under the advertising banner? The solution is often to retain such expenditure within the advertising and promotion budget because, as we shall see later, in the United Kingdom it is logical, permissible and advantageous to regard sponsorship as a form of advertising that qualifies for corporate tax relief. Most sponsorship organisations which are registered charities would benefit more from a covenant agreement, under which the donor agrees to give a certain sum annually for a period of time (reduced from seven to four years in the 1980 Budget). Most sponsors, however, are unwilling to commit themselves too far ahead, and a covenanted agreement may preclude getting much promotional mileage out of he association.

In 1974 a report prepared for the Royal Philharmonic Orchestra further defined sponsorship as 'the donation or loan of resources (men, money, materials, etc.) by private individuals or organisations to other individuals or organisations engaged in the provision of those public goods and services designed to improve the quality of life'. Two years earlier the Acumen Marketing Group had suggested that sponsorship was 'the provision of financial or material support (a) for some independent activity which is not intrinsic to the furtherance of commercial aims, but (b) from which the supporting company might reasonably hope to gain commercial benefit'.

The deficiency in the latter definition, as Nigel Waite pointed out in his Cranfield School of Management report *Sponsorship in the UK* (1977), is that, quite often, companies may support activities which are not independent of but are, in fact, intrinsic to the furtherance of commercial aims, such as a manufacturer of powerboats encouraging powerboat racing. The RPO definition, too, is questionable. For instance, whose life quality is being improved by the Olympic athlete enjoying a diet of beefsteak provided by a firm of butchers? It also overlooks any distinction between providing help with a view to getting some kind of return and giving assistance purely out of a sense of altruism.

Keith Diggle did some necessary clarifying in the *Guardian* (23 October 1975):

Patronage, by both definition and usage, is essentially an altruistic activity carried out with no expectation or return other than the satisfaction of knowing that good is being done. Subsidy is grant in aid derived from national or local government sources. Sponsorship, a term in common use where sport is concerned, implies a financial outlay with some form of material benefit as its primary justification.

This echoed the Sports Council's terse description in 1971: 'A gift or payment in return for some facility or privilege which aims to provide publicity for the donor'.

Diggle at least attempted to draw a distinction between sponsorship and modern-day patronage but the Economist Intelligence Unit probably came closer in 1977 with this stab at it:

The essential elements of the term sponsorship as it is used in the UK today are: (i) a sponsor makes a contribution in cash or kind – which may or may not include services and expertise – to an activity which is in some measure a leisure pursuit, either sport or within the broad definition of the arts; (ii) the sponsored activity does not form part of the main commercial function of the sponsoring body (otherwise it becomes straightforward promotion, rather than sponsorship); (iii) the sponsor expects a return in terms of publicity.

Interestingly, this comment draws a further distinction between sponsorship and promotion, under which latter heading the powerboat example referred to above would then fall. However, for practical (and tax) purposes, it is less important to make that definition than to observe the one made by Diggle between sponsorship and patronage.

In fact, many firms have been making this distinction for a number of years. It was felt to be confusing to include under sponsorship activities that should more appropriately be referred to as 'patronage'. Logically, this description was applied to straightforward charitable gifts for which no acknowledgment was expected or asked. Many dignified City institutions, which might blush at the thought of becoming involved in overt promotions, have been contributing substantial sums to charities for decades without drawing attention to it.

It is the expectation of something in return for one's money, be it even a modest mention of the company's name in a programme, that helps to identify the concept of sponsorship and separate it from patronage. Significantly more and more companies are adopting this distinction, regarding the two as quite separate activities to which different criteria apply. Pat Bowman's succinct summary in the 1987 *Guide* issued by ABSA (the Association for Business Sponsorship of the Arts) is: 'Charity is giving without thought of any reward. Patronage is supporting without any commercial incentive. Sponsorship is a commercial arrangement that is beneficial to both parties.'

Sponsorship can therefore be seen to include support of various kinds chiefly for sport and the arts, but it can also embrace such things as education, youth and environment programmes, and so on. Clearly it is not new. We have seen that the tradition of supporting of the arts has a lengthy history, and today's businessman may simply be inheriting a responsibility previously assumed by private patrons whose motives may not have been commercial.

What is undeniably new is the changing role of industry and commerce in society and the wider implications this has for sponsorship of any artistic, educational or recreational activity that can be said to nourish society. By accepting this responsibility a company acknowledges that what it is supporting is a vital ingredient of community life. Some, shy of the word 'responsibility' with its implication of duty, prefer to talk about 'opportunity' in this context. The arts, for instance, lie at the very roots of society, and to support them is to assist the development and cultural enrichment of society. The growing involvement of commerce, due partly to the diminution of wealthy private patrons, is largely a consequence of the re-affirmation of the wider role of commerce and its wish to contribute (and be seen to contribute) in another way to improving the quality of life.

If social responsibility is recognised as a fundamental reason for sponsorship, we can then describe the motivation for sponsors as enlightened self-interest. Pressure on companies to show that they are good corporate citizens is unlikely to diminish and, increasingly, businessmen, especially those who wish their companies to continue operating in a tolerant and tolerable climate in 10, 20 and 50 years' time, are acknowledging that they are part of the fabric of civilisation and must demonstrate a contribution to its improvement.

To acknowledge this interdependence of the various components of society is sometimes regarded as a weakness, but surely the reverse is true. Nor, by so doing, does a businessman contradict what, after all, should be the prime social responsibility of any company – to be successful and so protect the jobs of its employees, the welfare of its customers and the savings of its investors.

IBM's philosophy on arts sponsorship was summed up by its Chairman and Chief Executive, Edwin Nixon, when introducing his company's cultural sponsorship programme for 1979.

The growth of this programme reflects my view that a greater involvement by business in the mainstream of society is not only inevitable, but desirable. As society endures the tensions of modern life, the building of bridges between the different segments of which it is composed can only add to the stability of the whole.

It was encouraging to see that this philosophy continues; Nixon's successor, A. B. Cleaver, when delivering the Royal Society of Arts

Cantor Lecture in 1987 said: 'To assist in the creation of a prosperous and balanced society is not only good for society, it is good for the long-term future of industry and commerce'.

Similarly, David Maroni, Director of British Olivetti, explained his own company's philosophy: 'We are the sort of company that believes in involving itself in the community. When people look at a company, they judge it by its efficiency, its productivity level and its profits; but a firm's image should be more than just the sum of its commercial parts.'

For Johnsons Wax, Anthony Bracking, UK Director of Trade and Public Affairs, said, 'If we, and others like us, did not help in these sort of activities, the overall quality of life would be poorer and society at large would undoubtedly suffer.' Mr Bracking added, unforgettably, 'Johnsons Wax does not operate in isolation' and so reminded us that businessmen, like politicians (and journalists), can lapse into rhetoric. However, few will quarrel with his conclusion that 'We are part of a community and are intimately involved in the total environment around us.' How sponsorship can help translate this philosophy into reality and how firms can use it to bridge the chasms that often yawn between themselves and their various publics, national and local, is one of the lessons we can learn from the case histories discussed later.

The debate about social responsibility and business has livened up only comparatively recently in Europe, although it has been a familiar one in the United States for 30 years. Sponsorship is only a part of the debate, but an important part, and a would-be sponsor cannot ignore the wider issues involved.

Anyone interested in the survival of a Western form of free enterprise might consider the proposition that business must respond to pressures for social action, if only to prevent more state intervention and further erosion of the function of private enterprise in a mixed economy. This is to contradict Milton Friedman, who condemns the doctrine of social responsibility as 'fundamentally subversive' because it threatens the essential competitive nature of a free society. In a sense he echoes the old slogan 'the business of business is business' and supports the idea that the sole social responsibility of a business is 'to use its resources and engage in activities designed to increase its profits as long as it stays within the rules of the game, which is to engage in open and free competition without deception or fraud'.

All of this presupposes that corporate social action is taken only at the expense of profit. Somehow it is difficult to believe that profits are significantly diminished by any of the current programmes of social activity. Friedman's view carries even less weight when applied to sponsorship because social responsibility is only one of its motivations, as we shall see.

Certainly, one has sympathy for the opinion of Adam Smith who wrote 'I have never known much good done by those who affected to trade in the public good.' Indeed, as he pointed out, the entrepreneur, in pursuing his own gain, may, by chance, promote the interests of society more effectively than if he had deliberately set out to do so.

If all the money spent annually on sponsorships of one kind or another and on various charities, were channelled into wealth-creation, society might gain more material benefit in the long run. This, however, would not solve the problems of those arts or sports organisations that desperately need financial and other aid in order to keep going. It is a harsh philosophy that pronounces a death sentence on socially valuable pursuits which may not be commercially successful, and it leads inevitably to a society that, indeed, knows the price of everything and the value of nothing.

It is not too far-fetched to see a future connection between the electronic silicon chip and the subject of sponsorship. Microelectronics, like other great technological developments, such as broadcasting and air travel, will profoundly affect people's everyday lives. This, plus the gradual move towards a shorter and shorter working week, will challenge both government and industry to teach society how to use this increased leisure time without coming apart at the seams.

One constructive move in this direction would be to widen the appeal of the arts and increase the availability of sport to both player and spectator at prices that they can afford. This will continue to be a drain on government funds, and the opportunities will multiply for business to take a larger share of this responsibility.

The confusion that exists over defining precisely what sponsorship is can be seen in the attitudes of many prospective sponsors when they eventually decide to include it in their overall market strategy. This is probably because different sponsors have different priorities, and any sponsorship activity, whatever its objectives, may, at some stage, include elements of corporate advertising, marketing, press and public relations and internal communications. The sponsors may choose the wrong vehicle to promote themselves. They may expect high visibility from something that is essentially a low-profile event. They may fail to line up their target audience, omit proper research into the sponsored event, neglect the staff work that is vital in cementing an efficient relationship and, disappointed at not achieving quick responses, commit the cardinal sin of abandoning a sponsorship after a brief courtship and so lose any investment of time, money and goodwill.

Accepting this, there can be little doubt that, if properly planned and carried out with clear objectives in mind, a sponsorship programme can, over a period of time, benefit all involved and also the community as a whole. Among the commercial advantages for the corporate sponsor that we should examine in more detail is the offer of a sound medium for achieving product or brand visibility. It can also be a highly sophisticated means of projecting a favourable company face at selected audiences. The trick is to prevent this company 'smile' becoming an inane grin.

The variety of uses to which sponsorship can be put has plus and minus implications. It can be a marketing tool or a vehicle for public relations. It can enhance or alter reputations or public perception, strengthen loyalty, boost brand names, influence target audiences and open new marketing horizons. It can help to improve relations with staff, customers and shareholders and send messages to opinion formers in the media and government. But its effects are often long-term and difficult to evaluate. Small wonder that marketing and advertising men are only now beginning to lose their suspicion and mistrust of what they regarded as an irritating competitor, too small to take really seriously, but capable of diverting funds from the realities of commercial life. 'It's probably still true that we in advertising have not yet properly made up our minds about sponsorship,' confessed Roger Underhill, Director-General of The Advertising Association, to me as recently as the autumn of 1987. This contrasts with the experience in many other countries where agencies have quickly recognised the opportunities offered by sponsorship, although fewer clients have shown a comparable interest in taking part. Kenneth Miles, Director of ISBA (The Incorporated Society of British Advertisers Ltd) equates advertising agency scepticism with a fear of being criticised for recommending expenditure which cannot be validated. 'In most areas of marketing activity, an agency expects to produce valid facts and figures to back up its recommendations', he told me. 'But where sponsorship is concerned this is seldom possible and, therefore, the agency lacks the courage or experience to see how the benefits could accrue and could be measured. This implies a lack of imagination on the part of agencies, which may seem surprising since creativity and imagination are among their major assets.' No doubt on the 'If you can't beat 'em, join 'em' principle some agencies have started separate sponsorship consultancies instead of buying in specialist advice from consultants.

Even so, as if to contradict the general feeling, sponsorship is still depicted as a minor item on most publicity budgets, following such early studies as the 1976 Cranfield survey which from a limited cull showed only four companies then spending over £250,000 a year on sponsorship and only a dozen in the £100,000-plus bracket. The situation has been transformed since then but a decade later the Henry Goldberg study suggested that most sponsors were still spending on sponsorship only a small percentage of their total budgets for advertising, promotion and publicity. Levels of from 1 per cent to 5 per cent were common.

The truth can become obscured because sponsorship is treated differently by different companies. Some may have a separate sponsorship budget but retain the hidden costs in the advertising, publicity or promotion budgets especially when a sponsorship runs hand in hand with a brand campaign. And it is important to remember the difference between sponsoring sport and the arts. While support for the latter in Britain has increased sixfold since 1981, with an estimated £30 million being spent annually, it still lags some way behind sport in terms of financial backing. Sport is, of course, a much more obvious marketing vehicle, with greater likelihood of television exposure for the company name. It is unwise to expect too much visibility of that sort in arts sponsorship and, indeed, illogical to do so. The brand logo on a racing car flashing across the screen is fine, but on the jacket of Sir Georg Solti conducting the London Philharmonic Orchestra . . . ? Perhaps not.

It is difficult to measure, but I have a feeling that the company sponsoring a Royal Festival Hall concert who decided to set up its own trade display in the entrance lobby, albeit staffed by attractive salesgirls, may have done its image more harm than good. Concert goers do not appreciate having their pockets nudged or their attention distracted. The sponsorship message can be shouted in sport but, in art, a whisper is not only more appropriate but also more effective.

CHAPTER 2

History and development

Although we tend to think of sponsorship as a modern invention, it is not difficult to realise that it has its roots in ancient history. In some form or other it has always been needed to enable the talented and creative, whose skills did not have an obvious market, to concentrate on what they did best without starving in the process. Nor have a sponsor's motives changed much. The Roman patriarch who sponsored gladiatorial games may have done so for political reasons, to win public esteem and to protect the fortunes of his family. Similarly, a tobacco company today might pin its faith on a sporting or artistic event.

Gladiatorial displays were staged by victorious generals to celebrate their triumphs, but officials of every rank soon saw in them a useful means of achieving popularity. Functionaries known as aediles, for example, funded supplementary games (*ludi honorarii*) attached to theatre and circus performances. When Caesar, as aedile, put on a gladiatorial show in 65 BC in memory of his father, the publicity about his immense troop of combatants frightened political opponents into rushing through legislation limiting the size of such personal entourages that anyone might keep in Rome. Even so, his 320 pairs of silver-clad combatants completely up-staged his fellow aedile, and won Caesar many votes. Two years later the Senate passed a measure disqualifying from office any candidate who had financed such a vote-catching show during the two years immediately preceding his election. It is an intriguing thought that sports sponsorship by modern political parties may not be such a far-fetched idea.

Roman games, like popular modern sports, tended to expand at a rate that outstripped self-financing. They occupied 66 days a year in the time of Augustus, 135 under Marcus Aurelius, and 175 or more in the fourth century. Augustus sponsored three 'extraordinary' gladiatorial games (i.e. displays over and above the regular shows given by officials) in his own name and five in the names of his sons and grandsons. Such considerable expense and carnage involved no less than 10,000 fighters, and gave him a virtual monopoly of such entertainments and an almost exclusive right to the prestige they earned.

Trajan celebrated his victories in Dacia with four months of entertainments in AD 107, during which 10,000 animals and 10,000 gladiators were sent into the amphitheatre. Altogether, between AD 106 and AD 114, at least 23,000 gladiators were fighting under imperial auspices.

Gladiatorial entertainments eventually became an essential public service that an emperor had to provide in order to keep his popularity and his job. It had its disadvantages, since emperors themselves were expected to attend and thus became conspicuous, vulnerable, and liable to public pressures from which they were usually protected. This is why the games were unpopular with rulers such as Marcus Aurelius. Indeed, the spectacle, although a vast and popular imperial activity, carried a tinge of shame – a theme strangely unreflected in the vast, comprehensive range of imperial Roman coins.

Sponsorship of the games became so important that in 22 BC Augustus ruled that no officials other than praetors should organise such contests, and then only twice a year with never more than 120 combatants. However, elsewhere in Italy gladiatorial displays were constantly arranged by private individuals. Such local sponsors enjoyed considerable prestige during the event and could wear the insignia of a high official. As today, the rewards included a number of free seats and others to be hired out for profit, or as a contribution to some worthy public work.

City priests were among the sponsors, which would seem a strange feature of such brutalities, were it not for their religious origin. Ambitious businessmen as well as politicians joined in, and Martial is very caustic and snobbish about the low social status of some who succeeded in achieving this ambition, e.g. a shoe-maker at the cultured city of Bononia, and a fuller at Mutina (Modena). Nor were joint sponsorships unknown, for partnerships were formed to present costly gladiatorial fights.

The holder (editor) of a show used it chiefly to win popularity for electoral purposes. He bought or hired the gladiators, or commissioned a manager (*lanista*) to recruit and train his team. As now, the burden of financing this activity was shared uneasily and unequally at different times between the private sector and the State. Minimum rates of expenditure were fixed but sponsors could receive grants in aid, and local corporations might supplement available funds by private bequests or gifts contributed by individuals out of gratitude for election to municipal offices. Even so, the financial burden of giving gladiatorial shows tended to become intolerably heavy and Marcus Aurelius's Senate tried to reduce costs by establishing maximum sale prices for the various categories of gladiators throughout the Empire. It was a gesture towards the wealthy classes, whose support the emperor needed in a time of military crisis.

It would be inaccurate, of course, to describe the gladiatorial combat as 'sport', itself a term misused today since, strictly, it refers to country pursuits such as hunting and fishing. However, the Roman games are not all that far removed from some activities seen in modern sports amphitheatres.

Although modern professional boxing has until recently generally dispensed with sponsorship (DAF's sponsorship of world champion Alan Minter indicated the changing attitudes), the Regency prize ring admirably demonstrates the importance of sponsorship and its role in society. Prize fighting became a cult by the beginning of the nineteenth century in England, and its patrons included royalty, wealthy aristocrats and political luminaries such as William Windham and Lord Althorp. Its appeal was varied. True, like the Roman games, it ritualised violence, but it also captured the imagination and provided public heroes, sponsored by rich patrons, who became nationally famous, thanks to the publicity achieved in the newly expanding national press. The sponsors, in this instance, were not seeking fame or fortune so much as indulging their own personal tastes. No doubt, some achieved an identity and standing in the eyes of the *cognescenti* that they could never have done through birth, wealth or any other activity.

Although support for the arts has a long history, it is the game of cricket that provides us with one of the earliest examples of a sponsored annual publication. John Wisden, a gentlemen's outfitter in Worcestershire, hit upon the idea of sponsoring cricket's reference book to which he gave his name and that of the family firm. *Wisden's Cricketers' Almanack* is now in its 125th year of publication, and the family firm, still existing, remains its proprietor with a seemly advertisement on the back of each copy. Latter-day imitators have included rugby and football annuals, *Pear's Cyclopaedia*, the *Guinness Book of Records* and *The Hambro Tax Guide*, subsidised by the banking firm. Barclays, having taken over the English Football League sponsorship, now have their own annual *League Club Directory* and *Yearbook*, complete with chairman's message from John Quinton giving his bank's reasons for sponsoring football – 2,800 branches, one in every League club town, etc.

The sponsored book is, in fact, much more common in the United States and James Chesterman, who started his own firm Publications for Companies in 1970, estimated that they represent at least 10 per cent of all premium offers in the USA.

Literature has also depended, at times, on sponsorship, although the debt is obscured by Dr Johnson's definition of a patron following his experience with Lord Chesterfield. His appeals to Chesterfield for patronage during the preparation of the *Dictionary* had proved unavailing until ten hard years later. Then, when the great work was ready for publication, Chesterfield wrote two supporting articles. Enraged at such opportunism, Johnson sent the Earl this cool rebuke:

Is not a Patron, My Lord, one who looks with unconcern on a Man struggling for Life in the water and when he has reached ground encumbers him with help. The notice which you have been pleased to take of my Labours, had it been early, had been kind; but it has been delayed till I am indifferent and cannot enjoy it, till I am solitary and cannot impart it, till I am known and do not want it.

I hope it is no very cynical asperity not to confess obligation where no benefit has been received, or to be unwilling that the Public should consider me as owing that to a Patron, which Providence has enabled me to do for myself.

Having carried on my work thus far with so little obligation to any Favourer of Learning I shall not be disappointed though I should conclude it, if less be possible, with less, for I have been long wakened from that Dream of hope, in which I once boasted myself with so much exultation, My lord Your Lordship's Most humble, Most Obedient Servant,

Sam: Johnson

In Shakespeare's day acting companies could rely on less niggardly sponsors and they had the patronage of the Queen and various lords. In 1587 London boasted at least six companies, five called after noble patrons, and one after Elizabeth I, who showed Shakespeare special favour. Until the end of her reign, his plays were repeatedly acted in her presence.

Such favour continued under James I and, on 19 May 1603, soon after his accession, a royal licence was granted to Shakespeare and nine other actors

freely to use and exercise the arte and facultie of playing comedies, tragedies, histories, enterludes, moralls, pastoralles, stage-plaies, and such other like as they have already studied, or hereafter shall use or studie as well for the recreation of our loving subjectes as for our solace and pleasure, when we shall thinke good to see them during our pleasure.

The Globe Theatre was their home base, but permission was granted for them to go on tour. The company was then styled The King's Company, while its members became 'the king's servants'.

Such support was vital. Between 1591 and 1599 it is estimated that Shakespeare earned about £17 a year as a dramatist (for 19 plays). Fortunately, his salary as an actor – probably not less than £100 a year in 1599 – was a substantial income in a country town. As a shareholder of the Globe Theatre he received probably more than £500 per annum. His earnings as dramatist during 1599–1611 (for 17 plays) amounted to about £15 per annum, while extra court performances under James I and the additional royal favour may well have brought him in £20 per annum. Thus, gifts from patrons did augment Shakespeare's resources, although his income was largely due to his earnings.

It was said, though never proved, that the Earl of Southampton gave Shakespeare £1,000 to buy a house. However, Southampton's importance is as Shakespeare's literary patron (and his only one). Plague was making life difficult for the acting profession, and Southampton became Shakespeare's patron in that decisive period of his life and career (in 1592).

The poet-patron relationship is the basis of the *Sonnets*: they are sonnets of duty to patron with the tone becoming warmer as the acquaintance progresses. By 1594–95 the formation of the Lord Chamberlain's Company provided a safe income and, though retaining his affection for Southampton, Shakespeare could make his own way 'poor but free'. His debt to this relationship was increased sophistication with an introduction to cultivated society and artistic development through contact with the other arts, music and painting, perhaps the best testimonial of all to any arts patronage.

Music in England owes something to patronage, especially under Henry VIII, when a musician of first-rate ability would aspire to join the King's musicians. Such royal patronage was common throughout Europe, but England took the lead in the establishment of commercial concerts to which the public were admitted on payment. A special concert-room was constructed in London in as early as 1713 and so the old concept of patronage was weakened. It is ironic that the wheel has turned full circle and London concerts cannot survive without support.

Elsewhere in Europe, musical appreciation remained for a long time a privilege of the upper classes. Court opera in the eighteenth/nineteenth century was performed to an invited audience of courtiers, titled gentry, officers and officials. Princely patrons expected no reward other than aesthetic pleasure, the satisfaction of their guests and some added lustre to their standing. Competition, however, was intense and they sought to outdo each other in the magnificence of their theatres and the quality of their singers. Some small rulers, like Duke Charles Eugène of Württemberg, went too far. Duke Charles impoverished his country and outraged his subjects by trying to compete with the productions of larger courts, particularly the French.

Patrons not only paid the piper but tried to tell him how to play. Indeed, many were aspiring poets or composers and, therefore, absorbed in theatrical affairs. The Empress Maria Theresa and Joseph II in Vienna, Frederick the Great, Elector Max Joseph of Bavaria (Munich) and Elector Charles Theodore of the Palatinate (Mannheim) were all experienced producers and sought the services of leading Italian singers and librettists whom they appointed court poets.

By the middle of the eighteenth century court opera relaxed the social rules and admitted wider audiences. The rising costs forced them to do this since the courts could not meet the expenses. Some part of the outlay was passed on to the general public by charging admission fees or leasing to independent impresarios, or by reducing the number of productions in favour of subsidies to private theatres.

Handel is among the composers who received a helping hand from patrons, and the influence of the Prince of Tuscany, brother of the Grand Duke Giovanni Gaston de' Medici, had something to do with Handel's journey to Italy in 1707. In Florence his first Italian opera, *Rodrigo*, was a great success, and the Grand Duke rewarded him with 100 sequins and a service of plate.

Six years later Handel's ode on Queen Anne's birthday was performed in London, probably in St James's Palace, and his work known as *Utrecht Te Deum and Jubilate* was performed at St Paul's in celebration of the peace. The Queen was too ill to be present but the music was subsequently performed in her private chapel and she conferred on Handel an annuity of £200.

After Queen Anne's death in 1714, the accession of the Elector of Hanover to the throne of Great Britain put Handel in an awkward predicament. He was out of favour with the Hanoverian court, but his new patron, the Earl of Burlington, and an old friend, Baron Kielmannsegge, devised a plan to restore him to court favour. They persuaded Handel to write a series of instrumental movements which were played in a barge immediately following a royal river procession from Whitehall to Limehouse. George I was delighted and gave Handel a further pension of £200 a year and £200 as payment for musical instruction of the young daughters of the Prince of Wales.

Mozart's reliance on patronage is well documented, too. Salzburg was ruled by a Prince-Archbishop who, as head of both Church and State, offered virtually the sole patronage available to artists of any kind. Everything depended on his personal whim. Clearly, it was desirable, if possible, for an artist to seek alternative patronage elsewhere. When Mozart and his sister were children, their father Leopold got leave of absence from his post as Vice-Kapellmeister and Court Composer and travelled from court to court (Munich, Vienna, Augsburg, Aachen, Brussels, Paris, London, etc.) giving concerts.

In Vienna Mozart very much impressed the Emperor and in London he had a gracious reception at court. The King gave Mozart pieces by composers such as J. C. Bach and Handel to play by sight, and Leopold had six of Mozart's sonatas for harpsichord and violin engraved at his own cost and dedicated to the Queen who sent him 50 guineas.

Subsequently, Mozart's experiences with patrons were not always happy and, back in Salzburg in 1777, he found life intolerable; he was disgusted at the lack of appreciation of art, and relations with the Archbishop (Hieronymus) became strained. In Munich, although in great demand as a performer, he could not get a permanent appointment, and from 1778 he had to give lessons on the clavier or composition to keep from poverty. In 1787 the Emperor made him Court Composer in Vienna at a salary of 800 florins (about £80), but Mozart looked upon this appointment as a mere beggars' dole and, when sending in the customary sealed letter stating his income, he wrote: 'Too much for what I produce [viz. the dances for the imperial balls], too little for what I could produce.'

Haydn considered his most important works the big operas. These were composed for and lavishly produced by his patron, Prince Nicolaus Esterházy, who was one of the most effective and generous patrons. From 1776 to 1790 Esterház rivalled Naples, Milan, Vienna and Paris as one of the leading opera houses in Europe, and between these years Haydn conducted over 100 grand operas composed by himself and others.

Nicolaus had lived surrounded by music and theatre (in the form of strolling players) in a hunting lodge at Süttör and, immediately after he succeeded his brother as Prince Esterházy and moved to Eisenstadt, he commissioned Haydn to write a series of short Italian comedies and an opera. The Prince regularly engaged *Wandertruppen*, strolling players, who took up residence at Eisenstadt or Esterház. His troupe became famous. The Empress Maria Theresa told everyone, 'If I want to hear a good opera, I go to Esterház.'

The Prince enlarged his hunting lodge into a magnificent rococo palace (still standing today), and built comfortable quarters for the musicians and strolling players. A splendid new opera house was opened in 1768 and for one of the Prince's typically lavish spectacles – music, theatre, fireworks, banquets, balls and hunting parties – staged for the marriage of his niece in 1770, Haydn wrote the opera *Le Pescatrici*.

Of course, sponsorship, or patronage, was common to the eighteenth century in a wide range of activities outside the arts. It was essential for an ambitious youngster of the middle classes to obtain the right patronage. At a local level, tradesmen and small manufacturers, centred on market towns, were almost entirely dependent on the favour of the surrounding landowners. Josiah Wedgwood, who pioneered a mass market for domestic crockery, was desperately anxious to bring his wares to the notice of the nobility, the gentry and above all to the members of the Royal Family.

In much the same way that royal, clerical and other benefactors have endowed so many great educational institutions, private patronage has been responsible for the foundation of many other institutions. These include great libraries (for example the Bodleian at Oxford, and Manchester's Rylands Library), and art galleries, such as the Tate, built on the north bank of the Thames in London at the expense of Sir Henry Tate, and the National Portrait Gallery, constructed in 1896 largely at the expense of a private benefactor, Mr W. H. Alexander. There have been many more recent examples of private endowments of art collections, museums and galleries in the United States.

Individual artists have, of course, depended upon private patronage for centuries, and since the Middle Ages the Church has played a significant and, indeed, decisive role at times in the development and direction of painting. The coming of Protestantism no doubt reduced the demand (and financial backing) for religious pictures, and when monarchy took over the chief role of art patron this led, to some extent, to the rise of the portrait painter. Henry VIII, Charles I and later kings encouraged such foreign artists as Holbein, Van Dyck and Rubens, and, subsequently, Gainsborough and other painters developed under the auspices of patronage.

The most famous private patron of the High Renaissance in Italy was the Medici family. Donatello, Filippo Lippi, Fra' Angelico, Luca della Robbia all flourished under Cosimo and Piero, and Lorenzo became the patron of Botticelli, Leonardo, Ghirlandaio and Michelangelo. Lorenzo was more than a patron: he was a teacher, and he took the boy Michelangelo under his wing to live with his household. For 18 years the family accepted the artist as an adopted son, and Michelangelo gained a valuable education by associating with the great men that Lorenzo gathered around him. After Lorenzo's death in 1492 his son, Piero de' Medici, although friendly, employed Michelangelo on such unworthy commissions as a statue of snow and the artist wisely left his protection.

In Renaissance Italy the household system was one of the chief forms of patronage, under which a rich man would take an artist or writer into his house for some years, give him board and lodging and supply his artistic and literary needs. Another form was a personal relationship between artist or writer and his client that lasted only until the painting or poem was delivered.

Patrons were ecclesiastical and lay. Perugino painted an altar-piece of the Ascension for the monks of S. Pietro at Perugia; Botticelli painted *Primavera* for Lorenzo de' Medici. A form of business patronage was well established. The wool guild in Florence paid for the Cathedral, and the cloth guild commissioned Ghiberti's famous Baptistry doors. (A competition in 1400 for this commission saw Brunelleschi lose to Ghiberti.)

Religious confraternities and the State were also corporate patrons. The Confraternity of the Conception of the Virgin at the Church of S. Francesco in Milan commissioned Leonardo (and the de Predis brothers) to paint the *Virgin of the Rocks*. The Florentine government hired Michelangelo to make his bronze David (the marble one was for the Operai del Duomo, the Board of Works of the Cathedral). State patronage became particularly important in Venice, where Giovanni Bellini was appointed as Painter to the Republic in 1483 and Dürer was offered a similar position. Official portraits of the doges and also historical paintings of scenes showing Venetian triumphs were painted by Bellini and Titian.

Our own misgivings about the ethics of sponsorship, the fear of too much influence by a sponsor, were not shared by the patrons of the Renaissance, who were quick to express their opinions or dissatisfaction. Federico Gonzaga of Mantua wrote impatiently to Titian in 1531 asking for a picture of the Magdalen 'and above all, let me have it quickly'. It arrived in less than a month, with a letter saying that Titian had dropped everything in order to oblige the prince. Later Federico wrote again asking for a painting of Christ 'for September'.

Princely patronage conferred higher status, and permanent service at court meant relative security. As today, the risk of a sudden withdrawal of aid was ever present. When a prince died, the artist might well be dismissed by his successor. Nor, indeed, were artists free. Mantegna at the court of Mantua had to ask permission to travel or accept outside commissions.

Patronage of paintings and sculpture was inspired by three motives: piety, prestige and pleasure (for today read social responsibility, publicity and entertainment facilities). Sometimes piety and prestige were intertwined, hence the coats of arms and portraits of donors that occur in religious pictures. The tabernacle commissioned by Piero de' Medici is inscribed 'The marble alone cost 4,000 florins.'

The role of patrons and clients is illuminated by the texts of contracts and commissions, often formal contracts, attested by a notary. The price and even the delivery date were usually written into contracts, with or without sanctions for failing to finish on time. Michelangelo's contract for 15 statues (in 1501) prohibited his accepting any other jobs that would delay him; Raphael was given two years to paint an altar-piece and the contract included a swingeing penalty clause (40 ducats fine, which was over half the price) for not finishing on time.

Pope Julius II, it will be remembered, organised a Swiss Guard and enrolled Michelangelo to design the uniform. His three major artistic projects made Rome the world centre of art as well as religion. They were the construction of St Peter's Cathedral, murals by Raphael in the Vatican palace, and Michelangelo's ceiling in the Sistine Chapel. However, an important motive was self-glorification.

Conflicts between patrons and artists were common, the most famous involving Pope Julius II and Michelangelo over the Sistine Chapel. Originally (in 1505) the Pope commissioned Michelangelo to sculpt a gigantic marble tomb, with more than 40 colossal statues. Only one was completed – the Moses – before Julius changed his mind. Michelangelo protested and after a long wrangle Julius commissioned the Sistine Chapel painting. Michelangelo still wanted to complete the tomb and did not enjoy painting the ceiling.

I am still in great distress of mind, because it is now a year since I had a penny from the Pope. And I do not ask, because my work is not going forward in a way that seems to me to deserve it. That comes from its difficulty and also from this not being my trade. And so I waste my time without results. God help me!

Pope Julius visited Michelangelo frequently to check how the work progressed – too frequently, apparently, because they often quarrelled about when it would be finished. It finally took Michelangelo four and a half years, until October 1512. Michelangelo got 3,000 ducats for his Sistine masterpiece, and Raphael received 12,000 ducats for each of the three rooms that he painted in the Vatican. Said Michelangelo, 'I cannot live under pressures from patrons, let alone paint.'

Compared with modern business sponsors, the Church and aristocracy displayed a highly developed commercial sense. They wanted value for money and drove hard bargains that would be unacceptable today. Although, as patrons, they helped to sustain art and contributed to its development, they were cost-conscious and considerably underawed by the presence of genius.

The court of Milan under Lodovico Sforza was another centre of Renaissance culture and, therefore, of patronage. Leonardo da Vinci in 1482 applied to Lodovico, stressing not his artistic talents but his skill as a military engineer. His letter, still extant, lists such accomplishments as making bridge mortars and chariots, and ends 'in the 10th place' that he can also paint and sculpt. It must rank as one of the world's superior job applications. He got the post as court painter, military and civil engineer, producer and designer of theatrical shows, interior decorator and architectural adviser.

Leonardo's *The Last Supper* was not for Lodovico but was commissioned to decorate the wall of the refectory of the Dominican monastery of Santa Maria delle Grazie. The prior complained that two key figures, Judas and Christ, were missing. Leonardo said he had been searching for features fit for Judas, going to the criminal quarter for inspiration. He said he might well use the prior's head but had hesitated out of consideration for his feelings!

In the seventeenth century artists such as Rembrandt found inspiration in Amsterdam's distinctive character and patronage from its business sector. The new, red-brick houses contained, in Protestant bourgeois style, not devotional pictures, but portraits of the merchant, his wife and their children. This sturdy bourgeoisie also commissioned group portraits, landscapes, sea-scapes, or scenes of domestic life.

Down from kings and counts, Church and State, senators and praetors, the responsibility and opportunity of what we now call sponsorship, for whatever motive, has been passed on, until today it is, to a large extent, the business of businessmen. From being rather unwilling foster parents, they are gradually assuming a more assertive and decisive attitude towards the subject of sponsorship as they perceive the opportunities it offers. It is in their interests to do so, because the rewards are more tangible than the shadowy immortality that the Earl of Southampton's patronage of a budding playwright and poet has earned him.

CHAPTER 3

Finance and fund-raising

Larry Westland has a Messianic glint in his eye when he talks about the National Festival of Music for Youth of which he is Director. 'If we could increase the number of regional festivals to twenty and make the final festival a four-day instead of three-day event, we would involve 18,000 young musicians, 3,000 orchestras and other groups, and the jazz bands are so good that they deserve a special evening to themselves.'

His arguments are passionate and persuasive and his cause is just. He epitomises the man at the centre of the current arts dilemma – the theatre director, the music producer, the festival administrator – whose energies have to be divided between creating and running a worthwhile cultural event and finding the money to finance it. Often such people are not experts in the field of fund-raising and, indeed, there are so many different financial paths to follow that their bewilderment is understandable.

It is a reflection of the British way of doing things that the funding of both the arts and sport in the United Kingdom should be such a mixture of the official and the unofficial. Government subsidy, ungenerous by comparison with that in many other countries, is barely enough to maintain existing standards and leaves little for expansion or development, hence the constant search for additional help from commercial sponsors.

The consequences are both good and bad. If artistic organisations were totally dependent on the bureaucratic purse, this could lead to undue political influence on creative talent. On the other hand, the situation breeds, at times, unhealthy competition for the extra pennies, and the winners are not always the most deserving or the most in need.

A large company receives hundreds of approaches during the year, ranging from mass-audience, televised sporting events to tiny, local galas, seeking a donation of £50 for a half-page advertisement in a cut-price programme, run off as a charitable gesture by the neighbourhood jobbing printer. All of them probably receive consideration, but very few get more detailed appraisal, partly because it is impossible, and indeed illogical, to engage in an unlimited amount of sponsorship activity, and partly because the approaches share common faults of preparation. These preparation faults are discussed in Chapter 9.

Where exactly does business sponsorship fit into the overall financial picture? In the case of the arts its role is important, although its contribution in money terms is comparatively modest. Preserving Britain's cultural heritage is, after all, primarily the concern of government and local authorities, although one finds this difficult to believe when talking to some politicians and councillors. In making comparisons of this sort it is usually forgotten that such official funding is derived from taxes of one kind or another, and it is not too difficult to trace the money back to its original source, the pockets of private individuals who include every businessman in the country. Indeed, it is claimed that the Government takes more money from the arts in VAT alone than it provides through Arts Council grants. If one adds income tax payments by those employed in the arts, savings on unemployment benefits, plus the income and foreign exchange generated by tourists attracted to these shores by Britain's artistic heritage, then the argument seems even more powerful. The net cost to the Exchequer, if it exists at all, must be tiny.

A Parliamentary Under Secretary of State at the Department of Education and Science has ministerial responsibility for general arts policy, which should aim to sustain a high level of artistic achievement and increase the availability of the arts. This is also the effect, if not exclusively the object, of business sponsorship.

By far the largest source of money for the arts in Britain is the Arts Council which, at times, has shown surprisingly un-Olympian pique at the credit received by business sponsors. When, in 1980, the Arts Council was prodded by the new Minister for the Arts, Norman St John-Stevas, into handing out £25,000 to the Association for Business Sponsorship of the Arts, the smiles worn by one or two officials may have been a little fixed. However, over lunch soon afterwards, Sir Roy Shaw, the Arts Council's Director General, was unruffled and apparently without rancour. He has the academic's detachment and the patience of a politician. He may have recalled, too, that in a sense, the Arts Council itself was begat by private enterprise.

The Arts Council had its origins in the wartime Council for the Encouragement of Music and Arts (CEMA), which stemmed from a fund created by the Pilgrim's Trust. The fund attracted money from the government, which, considering that the year was 1940 when the national outlook was overcast, showed remarkable faith and vision. Smaller minds might have insisted that every resource be concentrated on survival and sandbags instead of symphonies.

CEMA's work proved so worthwhile that in 1946 a permanent body with a royal charter, the Arts Council of Great Britain, inherited its function and is currently receiving an annual grant-in-aid from the Treasury of approximately £128 million. The grant profile for 1986/87 was as follows:

Table 3.1

	£
Regional arts associations	24,639,399
Music	23,108,879
Drama	27,096,402
Dance and mime	10,352,478
Touring	7,083,636
Literature	480,550
Art	1,981,171
Film, video and broadcasting	96,432
Combined arts	1,750,100
Training	488,699
Education	249,044
Housing the arts	661,500
South Bank Board	8,758,000
Scottish Arts Council	13,584,350
Welsh Arts Council	7,775,000
	128,105,640

This money is disbursed in grants, guarantees against loss, bursaries and capital funding to a great variety of recipients. National and regional theatre, opera, ballet, arts festivals, art centres and exhibitions are all aided. There are also some organisations that are subsidised by the Council, which in turn use those funds to assist other bodies: for instance, the regional arts associations, the London Orchestral Concert Board, the National Federation of Music Societies, the Theatre Investment Fund and the Visiting Arts Unit.

So who can get money and for what purposes? Under its charter, the Council has a wide discretion in deciding who to assist but, broadly speaking, financial aid is offered both to organisations and to individuals active in the arts in both a fully professional and an adult sense. Organisations may be given either capital (for which the Government provides a separate amount each year) or, more commonly, a revenue subsidy for:

(a) a year's entire artistic programme;
(b) specified projects or events, either one-off or a programme of a given number of weeks, as in a major arts festival, or for a tour or other part of a longer programme;
(c) commissioning new work; or
(d) to help an organisation to distribute aid for agreed objectives.

Subsidy for a whole year's programme can apply to any organisation, from national drama, ballet and opera companies, regional theatres and orchestras to smaller drama or dance companies, jazz and contemporary music societies, exhibition galleries or museums, arts centres, community arts groups, magazines, publishers or specialised trusts.

The Council may also offer help towards research surveys, conferences, tours, special assignments or training schemes. It gives awards and bursaries for visual artists, playwrights, actors and actresses, theatre directors, theatre technicians, film and video artists, writers, composers, choreographers, designers and photographers. Special Council schemes are designed to assist in converting studios and to provide essential equipment, commission works of art for public buildings and sites, purchase artists' paintings and sculptures, stimulate specialised training schemes, subsidise recordings of new music, establish artists-in-residence schemes, and support publications which concentrate on the work of artists. The Council directly promotes its own art exhibitions.

In view of the size and complexity of its operations – and those who have had any dealings at all with the artistic temperament in whatever sphere will understand some of the less obvious difficulties – the Council does try to minimise the rules and conditions attached to a subsidy. Even so, being embraced by the Arts Council is usually a more demanding experience than any dalliance with a business sponsor. Such items as budgets must be approved, and the Council may ask for box-office results and half-yearly financial statements, together with annual audited accounts. The preliminary investigation is searching, and rightly so. The Council will ask many questions.

What is the money to be spent on? What is the artistic *raison d'être* of the company? What has it done in the past and what is the artistic programme for the future? Has it a coherent, convincing artistic policy? Importantly, what is the artistic quality? Then how accessible to the general public is the end result? Or to whom is the policy directed? If intended for the public as a whole, is it for a particular section, such as disadvantaged people or a single small community (as in the case of many festivals)? What is the policy for attracting new audiences, children and young people especially? Is there scope for audience participation? What is the geographical area served: is the work concentrated or spread; is there a touring capacity or is it centred in one place? Is there any educational or information service built into the programme? Information on policy will need to be supported by estimates of expenditure and income, including salaries, production costs, box-office income and so on. The Council will ask about the policy on ticket price, including concessionary rates for students and old people, and constitution, management and administration.

While the Council will not insist that its subsidy is matched equally from elsewhere, it does show much interest in the other sources of income. The Council, rather than financing expenditure, offers subsidy to cover a budgeted deficit. This deficit is reached after reviewing all expenditure and other income, including earned income from the public and from royalties, fees, television rights, local authority support, and contributions from private firms, individuals and trusts.

Although the Arts Council, like a business sponsor, does not dictate artistic policy, it does require as a condition of subsidy to have its own representative, in an assessorship capacity, on clients' governing bodies. This assessor is usually the head of the department concerned. (In private sponsorship it usually works differently: for instance, I became a member and subsequently Chairman of the London Philharmonic Orchestra Council, but only at the LPO's invitation, and the same process applies to other appointments in the fields of music and the arts.) What are the chances of obtaining Arts Council subsidy? Not very bright, one fears. The Council has little money not already committed and its grant from the government barely keeps pace with inflation.

Anyone connected with raising money for the arts in Britain must be an optimist, and the Arts Council can claim that in the past few years funds have been transferred into new areas: regional arts associations, touring, community arts, arts centres, awards and bursaries, small-scale drama companies, training schemes, jazz, photography, contemporary music and dance. Music's 1987 share of the total Arts Council grants was 18 per cent, three times the proportion it received six years earlier. Other lucky recipients included drama with 21 per cent (13 per cent in 1981), dance and mime 8 per cent (3 per cent), while literature 0.37 per cent (1.3 per cent) and art 1.54 per cent (4.9 per cent) seemed on the downward slope.

There remains a formidable problem even if you are fortunate enough to be given an Arts Council grant. The machinery of allocation requires a vast amount of information from existing clients that, each July, is studied, processed and discussed in detail with the organisation concerned. Panels, advisory committees, finance and policy committees then chew all this over before the Council finally decides how much should be allocated to each principal category of arts activity, such as music, drama, literature, community arts, visual arts and so forth, in this planning timetable. This unavoidable, time-consuming process is bad enough, but the Arts Council itself is handicapped by not knowing, very often until the last minute, exactly how much the government will be giving it in the forthcoming financial year. Such delay is almost as bad as not having adequate funds, since it makes it extremely difficult for the Council to do any serious forward planning of priorities, but, more important, it transforms planning into a gamble for client companies and, in the process, makes good housekeeping almost impossible.

Two other grant-aiding organisations operate similarly to the Arts Council, giving money to arts-related fields of work. The British Film Institute funds film and video projects and the Crafts Advisory Committee aids craftsmen and crafts projects. The amounts available from these sources are small in comparison with the Arts Council, but many arts organisations may find areas of their activity that fit the criteria for getting funds from these groups. The policies and categories of giving of both the British Film Institute and the Crafts Advisory Committee are set out in their annual reports, and these can be obtained direct from them.

Mid-way between these national bodies and the local authorities (an important and often underestimated source of support for the arts) are the regional arts associations, twelve in England and three in Wales. Not surprisingly, they tend to differ in their outlook and priorities, and it makes sense, if you need their support, to get to know your own association and its officers, and, ideally, involve yourself or your organisation actively in the work of your regional association so that you can guide its policy making.

This is the same commonsense advice one gives to new business sponsors, namely *get involved* with the company you are sponsoring don't simply sign a cheque, sit back smugly and expect the sunshine of public acclaim to bathe you in its golden glow. It won't. If the public approves, it will show its approval not loudly nor at once, but quietly over a period of years.

Other possible sources of income for artistic organisations are the Charities Aid Foundation and various Trusts listed in the *Directory of Grant-making trusts* which you should find in the local library. Among the well known ones are the Gulbenkian and Baring Foundations, which each dispense around £1.5 million per year for a range of activities including the arts/humanities. Again, the approach to them needs careful preparation and homework. Contrary to popular misconception, they are not geese producing numberless golden eggs; they are administered by small staffs who know their business and who are trying to make the most of relatively little money.

While the funding of the arts leaves much to be desired, it is undeniable that many of the financial problems that plague arts organisations are self-inflicted. Extravagance and mismanagement are by no means unknown and, in music especially, we are in an era of unprecedented inflation. Never have top artists been paid so highly.

Since Paganini and Liszt there have always been a handful of artists to command high prices, but now, concert managers complain, the level of superstar fees is creating a crazy showbiz situation that make a nonsense of normal budgets and may well harm the business of serious music. People such as Pavarotti, Solti, Horowitz, Joan Sutherland and Bernstein, among others, are the exceptions who probably are worth every penny.

A Pavarotti concert is less a musical event these days than an entertainment, with people paying to see the man rather than hear the music. At $100,000 an appearance this would mean a considerable increase in ticket prices, and so such artists – Horowitz worked on 80 per cent of the box-office takings – are often booked for special events, pension fund concerts, fund-raising occasions and so on. According to the *International Herald Tribune*, other musical superstars performing in the United States in the early 1980s would include Rudolf Serkin ($25,000 an appearance), with Sutherland and Leontyne Price in the same bracket. In the $15,000 range would come performers like Isaac Stern, Mstislav Rostropovich, Itzhak Perlman and James Galway. Since then, no doubt, their fees have at least kept pace with inflation.

When such a high level of fees begins to percolate through the industry the first sufferers are the symphony orchestras, who find themselves engaged in a bidding competition for leading performers. One orchestra spokesman commented:

Chicago or Philadelphia will be afraid that we'll have artists they don't have, so they'll jack up their prices. Then we in New York have to meet those jacked-up prices. Orchestra managers around the country are talking about it. What the hell can we do about those crazy prices? Perhaps we can get together and form our own union.

The Philadelphia Orchestra's annual bill for soloists and conductors had doubled by the early 1980s to about $800,000, and a similar picture could be seen in Europe, particularly at the leading opera houses. Some trace this influence back to Rolf Liebermann, who ran the Paris Opera backed by a $30 million subsidy and was responsible for raising the fees of top artists not only in his own house but all over Europe.

It is small wonder that, without sponsorship, the Royal Opera House, Covent Garden, would lose thousands of pounds each night. Higher prices mean dearer tickets. Sir Colin Davis, Musical Director, pointed out the unfairness:

We will have to put up prices perhaps by 18 per cent, which is a great shame. It means that those opera lovers who could *just* afford the tickets will no longer be able to come often. It is irrational that taxpayers' money should be given us in subsidy, that we then charge them maximum ticket prices, and tax them on top of that with 15 per cent value added tax.

An obvious economy is to reduce the number of opera performances and do more ballet, which is cheaper to put on. The result would be a reduction in the creative flow, fewer commissions for contemporary composers, fewer new productions and an impoverishment of the nation's musical and operatic life at a time of high public enthusiasm.

Colin Davis put things in some sort of perspective when, talking to Drusilla Beyfus of *Vogue*, he pointed out that the tail end of Concorde would pay for both opera and the theatre. 'Even aviation *aficionados* could hardly object,' he said, 'because Concorde is a real minority project since so few people can enjoy it.'

Compared with the Arts Council's £128 million government grant, the £39 million received (through the Department of the Environment) by the equivalent official organisation for funding sport, the Sports Council, is modest. The situation is, however, balanced by the much larger contribution from sponsors, who rightly regard sport as a more visible and, therefore, in many ways, a more immediately effective method of achieving marketing ambitions.

This does not help the Sports Council, which needs more than £50 million each year in the 1980s if it is to carry out properly its function of making sport available to all. The Sports Council's grants to individual sports for 1986/87 are shown in Table 3.2 and they total less than £8 million. In the past decade some changes have occurred. The number of sports benefiting has increased from 46 to 70 and the newcomers include flying, ice hockey, judo, skateboarding, trampolining and, interestingly, wildfowling. Among those not aided are chess, darts, polo and speedway.

Table 3.2   Schedule II — Analysis of current grants

	1986/87	1985/86
1. Current grants to sports	£	£
Angling	106,021	102,849
Archery	76,024	41,133
Association football	20,996	29,575
Athletics	216,573	187,106
Badminton	120,721	147,408
Ballooning	5,863	12,000
Baseball and softball	2,218	174
Basket Ball	228,608	149,533
Billiards and snooker	28,858	47,015
Bobsleigh	98,000	67,500
Bowls	98,916	73,003
Boxing	112,260	90,426
Canoeing	196,789	239,410
Caving	18,101	16,806
Cricket	160,007	138,447
Croquet	26,840	24,147
Curling	2,443	5,276
Cycling	332,084	184,374
Fencing	249,903	147,475
Flying	5,659	4,364
Gliding	85,158	88,426
Golf	61,768	59,533
Gymnastics	302,095	224,150
Handball	80,680	48,087
Hang gliding	32,328	29,113
Hockey (field)	289,954	265,567
Hockey (ice)	18,674	16,827
Hockey (roller)	16,437	12,634
Judo	278,403	279,052
Lacrosse	70,692	67,825
Land Yachting	12,819	14,767
Lawn tennis	78,834	54,128
Life saving	47,803	43,545
Martial arts	84,731	108,735
Modern pentathlon	108,691	68,483
Motor cycling	25,347	11,465

Table 3.2 (cont.)

	1986/87	1985/86
Mountaineering	88,331	82,825
Movement and dance	194,817	151,835
Netball	64,169	58,750
Orienteering	113,383	106,552
Parachuting	110,457	71,516
Parascending	33,979	12,650
Petanque	3,028	5,841
Racketball	11,750	7,500
Rambling	46,694	33,966
Riding	225,745	178,652
Rowing	439,850	382,546
Rugby League	88,409	105,931
Rugby Union	72,138	12,485
Sailing	321,262	100,215
Shooting	230,946	172,886
Skateboarding	6,056	2,565
Skating	236,541	174,349
Skiing	404,500	317,969
Squash rackets	260,452	187,786
Sub-aqua	75,410	97,338
Surfing	29,341	20,936
Swimming	95,602	135,826
Table Tennis	169,134	140,357
Tennis and rackets	2,500	500
Tenpin bowling	44,043	39,670
Tobogganing	62,000	32,206
Trampolining	24,518	15,342
Triathlon	375	—
Tug of war	15,638	6,787
Volleyball	182,075	162,481
Water skiing	178,192	166,300
Weight lifting	71,776	61,796
Wildfowling	32,710	23,498
Wrestling	133,077	77,545
Totals	7,770,196	6,247,759

The Council, an independent body established by Royal Charter in 1972, has overall responsibility for British sports matters, as well as domestic affairs for England (separate councils exist for Scotland, Wales and Northern Ireland). Many of its resources of time, money and energy are used to stimulate other bodies, such as local authorities and local clubs, to make the most of their own potential assets. Typical of this was the grant used in 1978/79 to promote a 'Football and the Community' scheme.

This was designed, in collaboration with 29 Football League and 10 Rugby League clubs, to enable local communities to share facilities at the clubs concerned. The total capital cost was around £2.7 million, with the Sports Council chipping in £1.7 million. Twenty-two of the capital schemes involved providing floodlit, all-weather playing areas, and others led to new indoor sports areas, the largest being in Birmingham where an interesting partnership included the Sports Council, Birmingham City Council, Aston Villa Football Club and Associated Dairies.

The Council has spent something over £1 million on new schemes in deprived urban communities, among other things to convert obsolete buildings, to provide sports equipment, to support sports leaders and motivators and to encourage sports among people of different ethnic origins.

When I talked to Dick Jeeps, Chairman of the Sports Council, it was easy to catch his enthusiasm and share his vision of the immense resources of natural sporting talent that exist in Britain but that have so far remained untapped. It still is not all that difficult to recall the young Jeeps I knew at Bedford Modern School, hovering impatiently at the heels of a rugger scrum, keeping up a fairly constant flow of advice and comment to his forwards, and occasionally kicking a backside or two to encourage more effort. This has proved invaluable training for his subsequent career, which has more than once required him to carry out the same technique, first as an England and British Lions rugby scrum-half, then as President of the Rugby Union and eventually as the chief executive of British sport.

As we shall see in Chapter 4, Sports Council aid is dwarfed by the amount of commercial money being pumped into sport, currently estimated to be in the region of £170 million annually. This figure is composed of varying amounts to different sports, ranging from the £70 million spent on motor sport to sums of around £1,000–£5,000 attracted by events like skateboarding or water polo. Other high-visibility sports that attract big money are horse racing (£5 million), lawn tennis (£5 million), golf (£5 million), cricket (£4 million) and professional soccer (£10 million). These estimates are approximate because the various surveys differ in method and result and not every company supplies figures of expenditure, or, indeed, gives accurate figures. Most would agree, however, that the 'visible' expenditure is often only half or even a third of the true amount spent on a sponsorship.

Compare this with a figure of £20 million that business can spend on what is called 'perimeter advertising', that is putting the company name or message on boards that surround the playing area at such events as soccer and cricket matches and motor racing meetings. In this form of advertising space can be purchased either as part of a sponsorship arrangement or independently. Costs will vary enormously, depending upon the position of the board – a behind-the-goal site might cost twice as much as a sideline position, perhaps £4,000 a match – and discounts may accrue from long-term arrangements or from having boards at more than one match on the same day, for example. The best site at Wembley for the 1980 Cup Final cost £14,600 and on that day something like £200,000 came from the 36 advertising boards around the ground.

It is probable that in a season at British soccer matches this form of revenue then produced around £2.5 million for the clubs and, of course, the sign companies. For sponsors of a particular event it was galling to see their visibility reduced in this way, and sponsors of cricket Test matches must have felt this acutely. The usual number of boards at a Test match was about 40 and the average cost was £2,000. This gave a return of £80,000 for perimeter boards at every Test, and even if a major cricket sponsor, like Cornhill for example, took all the boards, it would have cost them as much as they spent on sponsoring Test cricket in a year.

Horse racing is another money-spinner for sign companies, with an annual revenue of something like £3 million. The Grand National alone has on screen – television coverage is naturally the main object of the exercise – 28 manufacturers' brand names, yielding perhaps £500,000 over the three-day meeting. And it must be remembered that, on most occasions, there is no guarantee of television exposure. The wheeling and dealing that necessarily takes place is just one of the many subordinate activities that anyone involved in sponsorship must quickly learn and use to advantage.

Sometimes the best-laid schemes go wrong. You may do your research, establish over a beer with the television technician the likely scanning area of his cameras, and reserve for yourself precisely the right corner of the ground, only to find that, for that match, the local disabled people's club have been given permission to line up their wheelchairs just in front of your perimeter boards!

CHAPTER 4

Sponsorship of major sports

Broadly speaking, sponsorship falls under the heading of either sport or the arts, and it is a mistake to believe that the two are like dogs scrapping over a bone. In fact, at present there is no real conflict and, indeed, no contest, as anyone with a rational approach to sponsorship will agree. It is not a question of Tchaikovsky *or* Tottenham Hotspur, Covent Garden *or* canoeing. Such comparisons are empty. Each can claim its own excellence and no sponsor would expect to receive the same publicity from a concert as from a lawn tennis tournament. On the other hand, greater prestige in a key audience sector might derive from the concert than from the tournament.

The businessman shopping for sponsorship opportunities will have in mind various objectives, all to do with improving his company's performance and achievement. These may vary from maximum publicity, linked, perhaps, with a specific advertising campaign, to a low-profile exercise as part of an overall good-image maintenance plan. In the supermarket of sport he has an embarrassment of choice. Motor racing, with its soaring costs, attracts almost half the £170 million spent on sports sponsorship each year. Running a two-car Formula I team consumes around £8 million a year in direct expenses, and other top-liners, as we have seen, include horse racing and equestrian events, lawn tennis, golf, soccer, cricket, athletics, cycling and gymnastics.

It is easy to explain the boom in sports sponsorship in Britain that began in the early 1970s. It was then that the value of attaching a company name to an event title really became recognised. It was suddenly possible to buy a way into a prestigious fixture with an established public, such as a golf or tennis tournament or a show jumping competition, and then rename it to include either a brand name or the company name. Opportunities abounded for television or newspaper exposure and gradually the people buying sponsorship grew more sophisticated, built up their contacts, and were able to identify events with the highest potential for media coverage.

Sports organisers are themselves eager to co-operate with sponsors, they stand less firmly on their dignity than do their artistic counterparts (some might argue that they have less dignity to stand on) and, generally, they give sponsors a better deal. Similarly, sports reporters are more generous in acknowledging sponsors, taking the not unrealistic view that sponsorship is news and to ignore the fact is feeble journalism.

Bill Kallaway, among the first entrepreneurial sponsorship 'middlemen', has described sport's common appeal as being 'competitive, instantly understood, and accessible; it has little or no mystique; it has many folk heroes and no hidden language'. He is certainly right about it being competitive and accessible. However, anyone who has spent an afternoon at Lord's attempting to explain cricket to an American might not agree that it is instantly understood or that it lacks mystique!

In many ways sports sponsorship in Britain has developed somewhat lop-sidedly because of the overwhelming involvement of the big tobacco firms. Banned from television, they were forced by circumstance to channel huge promotional funds into other areas, and sport became the beneficiary. It was for them a backdoor method of advertising, much to the disgust of organisations like ASH (Action on Smoking and Health).

However, in December 1977 Denis Howell, then Minister of State, Department of the Environment, in a written reply to a Parliamentary question, announced details of a new government agreement with the tobacco industry which, although not unexpected, must have caused gloom in the board rooms of Imperial Tobacco and other companies. Apart from limiting sponsorship expenditure[1] and requiring prior consultation with the Minister for proposed new major sponsorships, the agreement drew up a code of practice that severely limited the exposure that a cigarette manufacturer could obtain. For example, one clause stated: ' Where the sponsor is aware that the event is to be televised, signs should be placed so as to minimise the possibility of "freeze-frame shots" having the signs in view for prolonged period, e.g. on cricket scoreboards.' This, added to similar restrictions, was rather like asking Mohammed Ali to enter the ring with both hands tied behind his back and promise not to bite his opponent.

It was not all that surprising, in the fullness of time, to read in the press that W. D. & H. O. Wills were pulling out of Hickstead show jumping after 20 years. At Hickstead they had been restricted under the new agreement to a maximum of six signs, each not exceeding

90 square feet. Hambro Life Assurance (now Allied Dunbar), who, according to Deputy Chairman Mark Weinberg (*Daily Mail*, 15.8.80), had been 'seeking a suitable opportunity for sponsorship for more than two years', took over and announced a world record £11,333 first prize. The shows at the Sussex course have always been televised and Cliff Morgan, Head of BBC Outside Broadcasts, said: 'It's wonderful news. The BBC has been associated with Hickstead for many years and to us it's the world's number one equestrian centre.' Would that the BBC's arts producers shared Morgan's commonsense!

The news story had a slightly nostalgic flavour for me. Back in the 1960s, when Wills first became Hickstead sponsors, I negotiated a magazine promotion with the tobacco firm on behalf of *The Field*, of which I was then assistant editor. We wrote up Hickstead (not uncritically) in the magazine, and Wills fuelled a sales drive during Hickstead week in which every spectator was given a copy of *The Field*. The man negotiating the Wills end of the deal was Bill Kallaway, then the tobacco firm's events manager.

Since those days equestrianism has established a remarkably important position in sponsorship earning around £2.5 million annually. It attracts £1.5 million per year in prize money alone. Almost all shows are sponsored, and the sport uses a professional agency, British Equestrian Promotions, which promotes and organises sponsorships and feeds profits back to the British Horse Society and the British Show Jumping Association.

This success story is all the more intriguing when one considers how few of the 12 million people who allegedly watch the television saturation coverage of the Horse of the Year Show at Wembley have ever actually sat on a horse. Hugh Thomas of British Equestrian Promotions made a valid point when he reminded me that the number of active participants has been growing at between five and ten per cent a year for the past 15 years. 'Every year some three million people ride a horse at least once', he claims. 'Mostly, they ride for pleasure, on holidays or at weekends, but all have at least some interest in the sport at top level.'

Colonel Sir Harry Llewellyn, when President of the British Equestrian Foundation, with a fine disregard for government sensitivity about tobacco advertising, described sponsorship as a 'cheap but dignified way of advertising'. Firms like Everest Double Glazing manage to extract the last ounce of publicity when horses bearing the company name actually win jumping competitions which it sponsors.

The multiplicity of commercial interests and the increasing professionalism of the sport have all had an effect, and the absence of British riders from the 1980 Moscow Olympics, albeit in response to Mrs Thatcher's advice, was also a convenient opportunity to 'buy time'. Britain's desire to eliminate 'sham-amateurism' probably led to a readiness to issue professional licences, not emulated by other countries. The 1976 Montreal Olympics saw Britain lacking her most successful and experienced riders, but by the 1988 Olympics the wheel will have turned full circle with most British 'professional' showjumping riders reclassified as eligible for the Games.

From a sponsor's viewpoint, the appeal of equestrianism has something to do with its capacity to attract attention, whether it be Harvey Smith giving a Churchillian salute to officials, or Princess Anne obligingly taking a header into a ditch for the posse of press photographers and then perhaps offering a few unregal comments for the waiting reporters.

Quite apart from the big events, such as the Royal International Horse Show, the Horse of the Year Show and the Christmas Olympia Show, the BSJA runs almost 1,000 county events whose organisers can offer sponsors access to a public geared to Thelwell's 'pony club' audience. There are also more esoteric horse competitions, such as Three-Day events and dressage, which invite attention quite out of proportion to the numbers of active participants and often have the added piquancy of a royal involvement if this is considered important (and I have yet to meet an honest sponsor who does not admit that it is). The one occasion on which I can recall the Queen visiting our office in the City was when we were sponsoring the British Three-Day event team and held a reception for the riders and officials. Needless to say, Princess Anne also came along to support the side.

An academic inquiry into the appeal of equestrian events for sponsors would probably reveal that the horse itself is the basic lure. After all, a horse seems to embody many of the virtues that industry is attempting to project in its public image: it is reliable, handsome, honest, strong but not savage, peaceable but not apathetic, and even its waste products are instantly useful.

Horse racing has an obvious appeal for tobacco groups and the drink and bookmaking industries. However, when in 1975 the Jockey Club decided to allow companies to own horses, the gates opened much wider and among the early starters was the building firm Marley with a horse called Marleymix. Although he won a few races, Marleymix was no world beater on the track, but he certainly became a winner in the promotion sphere. He was bought for £3,000 as a three-year-old and cost a similar amount each year to keep and train. Marley described the investment as 'extremely good value' as a vehicle for publicity in the press, and on radio and television. 'At one meeting at Kempton Park in 1978, televised by the BBC, an estimated 3.5 million people saw the horse and heard the name many times,' said an enthusiastic spokesman. Marleymix ran in the same colours as the firm's products, a black and red chevron on yellow. 'This is all part of brand identification and has the dual effect of attracting both trade and consumers. And the actual name 'Marleymix' promotes the name of both the company and its range of instant concrete mixes. We, in fact, regard Marleymix as an equestrian addition to our public relations department.'

'A day at the races' is also used by companies to foster customer relations, perhaps to do a little new business, and also as a fillip to staff morale. The phrase has a fine ring to it but, without careful planning and on-the-spot supervision by the public relations department, the actuality can prove a disaster.

Many years ago a friend, who was heir-apparent to the chief executive of a Midlands industrial firm, had the bright idea of taking some important clients and their wives to Royal Ascot. The chief was delighted. 'Brilliant idea, my boy. Never been done around here before. Go ahead and fix it.' An open-roofed London bus was booked as a private grandstand in the centre of the course to view the racing, a champagne and salmon buffet was laid on and a coach was hired to convey the chairman and his guests down south. My friend was at the factory gates at 8 a.m. to wave them off in their grey toppers and Ascot dresses.

Next morning he was summoned before the chief executive whose expression was not friendly. Nothing, it seemed, had gone according to plan. The coach from a local firm had evidently been used earlier that morning to transport nearby colliery workers to the dawn shift. The ladies' finery and gentlemen's morning suits now required costly renovation and the chief had agreed to settle all dry cleaning bills. The coach driver, a youngster of unquenchable optimism but, alleged the chief, not quite right in the head, had never travelled south of Derby before and got hopelessly lost near Buckingham Palace. He eventually arrived at Ascot in the middle of a downpour, having missed the big race and too late to drive across the course to the central reservation. Chief executive and guests had to footslog through ankle-deep mud for three-quarters of a mile trying to identify their omnibus. To rub salt into the wounds, my friend's instructions had gone astray and, instead of the company name on the coach, it bore his own patronymic, properly hyphenated in splendid gold capitals, on a royal blue banner. Alas, the party was so late arriving that the catering staff had consumed all the food and, judging by their boisterous welcome, most of the champagne, too. He never did become chief executive of that company.

This tragi-comedy took place long before 1972 when Bovis started its Bovis Stakes at Ascot to give the staff a day out. Doubtless Bovis organised things rather better. Massey Ferguson, another company outside the traditional breed of sponsors, ran a prestigious race, and one of the most committed sponsors on the turf was Trafalgar House Limited, which actually went through the card at its sponsored meeting at Sandown. It was the only British enterprise to sponsor all six races on a full day's racing card. Trafalgar House described the event as being primarily for client reception, and they felt it promoted much goodwill for them over the years.

Clearly, the reported disillusionment of Colt Cars, who are said to have put up £77,000 (excluding the hidden costs) for the Grand National and felt convinced that they didn't get anything like their money's worth, is not shared by others, who perhaps identified their targets more accurately. Subsequently, the 'greatest race in the world' found a long-term (ten years from 1984) sponsor in Seagrams.

However, horse-racing sponsorship can be quite modest, individual races costing anything from a few hundred to several thousand pounds. Among those who have gone for the bigger events are Ever Ready Batteries (The Derby and Oaks, £1.8 million over three years), General Accident (2,000 and 1,000 Guineas), Holsten Pils (St Leger) and De Beers (King George VI and Queen Elizabeth Diamond Stakes).

Motor racing can claim to be the most sponsored of sports, receiving something approaching £60 million annually. Cars are part of most people's everyday lives and such familiarity is a big asset. The sport's variety of activities can fit most requirements and budgets. Not everyone is anxious to spend £7 million on sponsoring a team of Grand Prix drivers but, from that pinnacle, the scale of opportunities descends to sponsorship in kind, whereby technical aid or free parts may be supplied by tyre, fuel or components companies in return for fairly modest acknowledgements on car bodies, helmets or racing clothing. Public interest in motor sport draws vast crowds to Silverstone and healthy numbers to grass-roots club meetings.

The principal motives for sponsoring motor racing are wide ranging – as indeed are the motives behind any kind of sponsorship – and the RAC Motor Sports Association Ltd identifies them as:

(1) the massive advertising potential associated with increased television coverage of the sport at all levels;

(2) to obtain coverage for a product which is subject to restrictions on conventional advertising, e.g. tobacco (Camel and Marlboro);

(3) to cash in on the 'international jet set' image of the sport, for example drinks (Martini);

(4) to get a name, unassociated with the motor industry, better known among a wider audience, for example Canon;

(5) to add an element of glamour to a service or product which is not so associated;

(6) to become associated in the minds of motorists with the success and image of racing by providing a product used in the sport, e.g. tyres (Dunlop, Goodyear), heaters (De Longhi) and petrol (Shell, Texaco, Mobil);

(7) to use the sport and its facilities as a means of business or corporate entertainment;

(8) to satisfy the ambitions of an enthusiastic patron who is able to use the company he is associated with (or even owns) as a vehicle for funds;

(9) to satisfy nationalistic pride.

In practice, the picture is not as clear-cut as this, but the list does give an indication of what most companies expect to achieve through sports sponsorship.

Association football is Britain's most popular national game. In England alone, according to Football Association estimates, more than one million people play soccer, not including the services and schools. Each Saturday, 750,000 people watch Football League games, and weekend television soccer programmes command an audience of ten million.

Many people may be surprised to learn that it took the soccer authorities some years to accept the idea of sponsorship and when they finally did so the sponsors themselves were beginning to have second thoughts about associating themselves with a sport that was generating so much unsavoury publicity. Terrace hooliganism was already giving soccer a bad image and then came the terrible disasters of Bradford and Heysel. After the Heysel tragedy England was banned from European football competitions; it would have been more seemly had the English football authorities withdrawn voluntarily. The two clubs involved, Liverpool and Juventus, are working to bring about reconciliation. An Italian domestic appliance firm, Candy, signed a £1-million sponsorship deal with Liverpool in January 1988 and both sides described it as another bridge-building move. Ironically, Juventus are sponsored by Ariston, one of Candy's chief commercial competitors.

Despite the fact that alcohol has been banned from some grounds because of its links with terrace violence, breweries have been willing sponsors. Now all English Football League teams are sponsored to some degree and many minor competitions as well. A typical high-flyer was the £750,000 three-year deal between Tottenham Hotspur and Holsten, the international brewing concern, whose name appeared on the shirts of Spurs players. Their large advertising hoardings were strategically placed at White Hart Lane, the Spurs ground, to catch the press and television cameras.

Other companies can sponsor any of the 30 or so home matches at £4,000-plus per time for which they get the use of the sponsors' lounge to entertain up to 50 guests to lunch and seats in the stand near the directors' box. In addition, Tottenham had 72 executive boxes incorporated in a new £4.2 million grandstand which companies hire at up to £14,000 per season for entertaining clients. Sponsor-linked marketing and promotion efforts could boost the club's income from this source to around £2 million.

In the first edition of this book I speculated about the possibility of the English League itself being sponsored by someone willing to pay the huge price for having the league named after his company. My fears that the competition would first have to be broken down into smaller divisions with perhaps a super league at the top, were unfounded. Events have shown that Canon, *Today*[2] and later Barclays were only too happy to take on this project at around £3–4 million over three years. And following the now almost forgotten Texaco and Watney Cups, there has been an abundance of similar knock-out events – Milk Cup, Littlewoods Cup and Sinod Cup, enabling some clubs (Luton being a happy example) to tread the turf at Wembley three times in a season. Overkill? Maybe, but one trophy has so far resisted the sponsor – the FA Cup itself.

There have been narrow shaves, notably in November 1987, when the story broke that the FA were to sign a three-year £12-million deal with the Australian brewers of Fosters lager. One report claimed that it could be worth £20 million over four-and-a-half years. This was at odds with the words of Ted Croker, FA Secretary, whose recently published autobiography contained this stirring declaration of faith: 'We feel it (the FA Cup) is an event of such standing that it is above sponsorship. It generates enough money for football, some

£3.6 million a year, without needing an outside stimulus . . . Also, once you accept money from sponsors some of the magic would disappear.'

When news of the Fosters deal was leaked, the FA were said to be furious and it brought upon their heads an avalanche of protests from outraged fans. Was nothing sacred? Rogan Taylor of the Football Supporters' Association voiced the general concern: 'The FA Cup does appear to be the last bastion of the old values – the Virgin Mary of trophies, really – and it does seem a pity to sell it down the river'. The upshot was that no deal went through and, for the time being at least, the FA Cup remains pure and unsullied.

It would be heart-warming to think that public opinion persuaded the FA to refrain from making a deal worth £20 million, including the Charity Shield. But perhaps the decisive factor was the sponsor's wish to rename the historic trophy the Fosters Cup.

Professional cricket owes more to sponsorship than it may be prepared to admit. Not so many years ago it appeared moribund, stifled by the three-day county championship that aroused a storm of apathy among the paying public. I remember reporting county games at which the spectators were almost the proverbial 'man and his dog'. Even Test matches against Australia began to lose their glamour.

Then came abbreviated, one-day cricket, sponsored by companies like Player, Benson & Hedges and Gillette; interest quickened, and the colour returned to the patient's cheeks. The Prudential World Cup, Cornhill Tests and so on were the natural successors and, in the same way, so was Packerism and the Barnum and Bailey exploitation that followed.

Cricket is now saturated by sponsorship approaching £4 million a year and few attractive opportunities remain that offer benefits both to the sponsor and to the game itself. When I managed the group communications division for an international insurance company, Commercial Union, we were offered deals, involving touring sides both in England and overseas, that had such potential but which, for various reasons, did not fit into our sponsorship pattern. One that did, however, was a scheme for fostering young talent at schoolboy and apprentice-professional level. Ted Dexter, the former England Test captain who now runs a sponsorship consultancy, outlined his ideas for a Renaissance of English Batting, starting at the grass roots.

At that time England was going through one of its regular periods of batting uncertainty, and Ted's idea involved monthly awards for young county batsmen, a batting school at Lord's presided over by seasoned campaigners and, best of all, the re-flowering of an under-16 county championship with matches in all parts of Britain (incidentally, Commercial Union has offices in most sizeable towns). The idea of finding another Compton was the icing on the cake! Since it was aimed at *English* cricket, it was offered to the UK division. Among England Test players who benefited from this early encouragement are Mike Gatting and Graham Dilley. I mention this episode because of a personal involvement, but it is only fair to emphasise that Whitbreads have been by far the most consistent long-term sponsors of grass-roots cricket and generations of young cricketers can trace their early encouragement to Whitbread schemes.

The CU championship was a low-cost exercise that received coverage on the national sports pages and, more extensively, in provincial newspapers, which focus on local boys doing well at national level. More important from the sponsor's point of view was that it involved branch and regional staffs, helped to cement their relationships with local communities and, in a practical, wholesome way, reinforced a company image of care and involvement.

Part of this youth cricket sponsorship was international. For example, we sent two under-19 England teams to the 1979 International Youth Tournament in Toronto. Neither won it, but the Canadian office pushed out the boat for the youngsters, even hiring a Macdonald's double-decker bus to take them on a trip to the Niagara Falls. And hamburgers figured prominently on the menu!

Possible international involvement dominated discussions with Ted Dexter and his partner, Rayner Blanch, at regular meetings to consider sponsorship developments. This led us to the first ever junior world cup for under-18 golfers which we began up at St Andrews in September 1980 (see Chapter 8).

Sponsors in search of maximum publicity will find professional golf an expensive but effective vehicle that has a successful track record on television. Prize money at tournaments in the United Kingdom exceeds £5 million each year and does not represent the cost of, among other things, administration, publicity and entertainment, which can more than double the bill.

Martini's international tournament became established in the same way that the Piccadilly did, but the game also offers opportunities for off-beat sponsorship that can earn publicity in excess of the amount of money spent. One of the most publicised sports incidents of 1979 was the hole-in-one sunk by Japanese golfer Isao Aoki in the Colgate (formerly Piccadilly) World Match-play Championship at Wentworth. What gave it worldwide attention was the £40,000 Bovis home beside Gleneagles that was the special prize for Aoki's 'ace'. This appeared to be an expensive gamble by Bovis, but observers noted that a bet had been placed before the competition began with a firm of national bookmakers, who quoted odds of 40 to 1 against the hole-in-one. The anonymous punter put on £1,000 at those odds, so the chances are that that blast of international publicity cost Bovis a mere £1,000 (plus betting tax). In fact, it is possible to take out a straight insurance against such an eventuality and, depending upon the length of the hole and the calibre of the players, the premium on a £40,000 prize would be around £1,000.

One of the most popular golf programmes on British television is a series called 'Pro-celebrity Golf' in which a brace of professionals, like Ben Crenshaw and Lee Trevino, partner stars of stage and screen and other sports over six of the more photogenic holes at Gleneagles or some other lovely Scottish course. These matches are filmed during the summer, canned, and fed to the golf-starved millions in the long winter evenings, providing massive television coverage for the sponsors, latterly Waterfords.

Marley were among many to use golf as a way to entertain (and, hopefully, to impress) important clients. At one of its international challenge matches, in which Johnny Miller and Severiano Ballesteros played Tony Jacklin and Brian Barnes, 700 guests included customers for the whole range of Marley products as well as a fair proportion of pressmen. Guests had the benefit of watching four top golfers in action and later of participating in a golf clinic compèred by the former Ryder Cup golfer, Peter Allis, now a television commentator who also presides over the 'Pro-celebrity Golf' series. 'The event created a great deal of goodwill,' commented Marley, pointing out that more than 12 per cent of the British population play golf and many more take a keen interest as non-players, which makes it an ideal choice for company sponsorship.

Not all golf sponsors are so fortunate. Sun Alliance, who invested more than £1 million in the sport, was described as one of the unluckiest sponsors. The company took over the European Match-play Championship which in 1976 went to the King's Norton club, a relatively new course near Birmingham. Its television coverage was patchy, but when the new champion, Brian Barnes, was asked whether he liked match-play golf, his alleged reply was that he hated it and preferred to go fishing, which did not endear him to the Sun Alliance promotion department. In 1979 the Sun Alliance championship was not scheduled for television, but the Ryder Cup with which it was involved, due to be transmitted live in the September, should have compensated handsomely. Unfortunately, a technicians' strike scuppered those hopes and filmed highlights transmitted later in the year, late at night, were scarcely adequate recompense.

One of the dangers of 'pro-celebrity' golf is that it very easily loses its competitive appeal and therefore its credibility. The Phoenix-sponsored man *v.* woman series was a non-event competitively but, because it was shown during a Christmas holiday period, it scored reasonably high viewing figures. However, if the public do not believe in your sponsorship, this will not help them to take you seriously in other ways.

Sponsors can always remember 'the ones that got away' but, like the agent who turned down the Beatles, they do not always talk about them. But I was delighted when a British firm provided the winning bicycle of the Tour de France for the first time in July 1980, even if Commercial Union had declined a co-sponsorship seven years earlier. We turned it down because, on the Continent, where cycling has most impact, we did business largely through subsidiary companies and agents, and the need to put over the company name is less urgent. Tube Investments, the Raleigh cycle company with whom I discussed the idea, went on to spend £1,500,000 to ensure ultimate success in the prestige race and hoped to double European sales as a result.

Raleigh created one of Europe's most successful sponsored cycle racing teams and, at the same time, its own best publicity machine. Racing is, of course, the obvious publicity platform for cycle manufacturers but a Commercial Union involvement would not have seemed out-of-place, judging by what happened during the 1970s.

Blanket television coverage of European professional cycling during those years attracted hundreds of companies not connected with the sport, and the money they now invest in it is enormous. The story was that the only person in France who could sign a million-franc cheque without consultation with another person was Guy Merlin, head of a holiday homes building firm that had achieved its publicity from cycling, chiefly the Tour de France. His main contribution was to present the Tour winner with a £12,000 holiday apartment, and he got extra mileage by persuading the race organisers to start or finish various Tour stages at coastal resorts such as Merlin-Plage and Merlin-Aquitaine.

Lawn tennis, being such a natural television sport, has never been short of support for the big events, although many long-established and worthwhile tournaments have declined because they cannot afford the huge fees now demanded by top and not-so-top players. However, in many ways, lawn tennis provides the most disturbing examples of the adverse effects of sponsorship.

Commercial Union was among the first of the major sponsors when it took over the international Grand Prix in 1971 and ran it for five years. The Grand Prix is the overall men's championship and all the important tournaments, including Wimbledon, are part of it. It thus has the advantage of being international, long-running and a natural for television. The Grand Prix was just two years old and struggling when Commercial Union took it over and built it into the mammoth affair it is today. The sponsorship coincided with a need to get the company name known in the United States, where this British company had been doing business for a century but through various subsidiaries.

All the United States companies were being re-named Commercial Union, and tennis provided an excellent means of putting the name before a mass audience. The cost was then around £100,000 per year, but the bill has since gone up 20 times. Since this agreement was signed before I joined Commercial Union, I can say without blushing that it proved to be a bargain. One commentator said that CU was receiving millions of pounds worth of publicity for about £100,000 per year.

Although the Grand Prix achieved a satisfactory measure of success in terms of identification, it became increasingly less enchanting as the behaviour of some tennis stars deteriorated while their fees and prize money went higher and higher. The late Patrick Campbell summed up this disenchantment in one of his essays: 'Wimbledon, the Mecca of this so-called sport, has become an American slum with ex-ball-boys from Los Angeles making violent public scenes about decisions arrived at by British umpires of impeccable military antecedents, while egregious commercial elements write five-figure cheques in the dressing rooms.' This was written before John McEnroe's arrival.

Once, sitting in the office at a Grand Prix Masters, Ilie Nastase turned to me as a representative of the 'egregious commercial elements' and asked how much he would win if he beat his opponent in the match about to start. I told him that it would be about £25,000 and translated this into French francs. He whistled incredulously. Then a little-boy grin spread over those wolfish features. 'Jeesus,' he said, 'I'd better start taking this seriously – no?' In fact, I never doubted that Nastase already knew to the last penny what he would be getting, but such vast sums were, in those days, still something for him to wonder at. Talking about it to strangers was, I suppose, akin to grabbing handfuls of gold doubloons and allowing them to pour through his fingers.

Lawn tennis sponsors are often accused of pulling out without giving proper notice, but CU announced its intention of discontinuing the Grand Prix involvement at least a year ahead of time and there was some competition to succeed us. Although we pulled out of professional tennis, we retained some connections with the game, supporting the schoolboys' and schoolgirls' national championships. In 1979 we started the first-ever international umpires' courses, which were run by the official bodies for umpires and referees and which attract participants from all over the world, especially from the new nations of Africa and the Far East, where the game is in its infancy.

Best of all, the company maintained excellent relations with the All England Club and these produced several benefits, the most significant being the offer of a marquee for entertaining clients at Wimbledon during the Fortnight. It may seem odd today, but then the very idea of a commercial marquee within those sacred precincts seemed faintly irreverent to many people. The site we were given was one of the outer courts and its surrounds, and it is easily the largest at Wimbledon today. The following two or three years saw Commercial Union joined by other marquee owners like ICI, Wilkinsons, and Colgate, which took over the Grand Prix. The Club quickly recognised the gold-mine it possessed and the late Bagnall Harvey (followed by the Mark McCormack group) was hired to work the seam.

Wimbledon remains an important area for CU business promotion and entertaining, although the company withdrew from the Grand Prix years ago. One of our first steps was to take a five-year reservation on the site paid in advance – and this included an option to renew. Had we wished, we could have sub-let the entire marquee, portions of it or days' use of it during the Fortnight several times over because, although more than 100 marquees are used today, most are smaller and more limited in scope. More than 130 people, chiefly customers, business connections and opinion formers, are entertained each day to lunch and tea, and many are given seats. Marquee-holders automatically receive a ticket allocation, and one of my preoccupations in the early days was to acquire debenture Centre Court seats as they became available. We thus had a guaranteed supply from such sources over the next few years at an average price of £17 per ticket per day. A Centre Court ticket changed hands for £600 on Finals Day in 1981, and few can predict what the price will be in 1991.

Because of this long association with Wimbledon the organisers felt able to discuss problems with us. For instance, we debated ways of streamlining the annual ticket lottery, and this was investigated with advice from CU's computer experts. No, it did not give us an inside-track on lottery tickets. Like everyone else, we still painstakingly filled in an entry form, and each year we acquired a handful that way to boost the debentures already purchased. Something like 29 per cent of lottery ticket applicants are successful and each year Wimbledon returns cheques valued at around £1 million to the unlucky ones. I feel sure that most people would prefer their cheques to be put on deposit instead of gathering dust for three months in some office safe until the lottery takes place in April. The interest could go towards benefiting the game at grass-roots level, providing some of those all-weather, indoor courts that Britain urgently needs if its young players are ever to compete equally with American contemporaries blessed with Californian or Florida sunshine all the year round.

Will Wimbledon's officials ever succumb to total sponsorship? It is a possibility, but a remote one. They have resisted many offers over the years, including one of £1 million a year from a whisky firm. It is a delicate balancing act to extract as much money as possible from the various semi-sponsorship activities, such as the marquees, without going too far down the road of commercialism and destroying Wimbledon's unique character and special appeal for sponsors. They lost a certain amount of respect by failing to apply stricter discipline to McEnroe in 1981, and the decline in the player's behaviour on court in subsequent years can be traced back to this.

Athletics, with about £3 million coming in from business sponsorship, is reaching saturation point while the sport retains its present form. Its attraction as a television spectacle is reflected in the BBC's eagerness to sign a £1.5 million contract for rights covering the first four years of the 1980s. With other channels competing, the price has soared to £10.5 million for five years. Sponsorship opportunities vary from funding a costly major televised tournament (£100,000 plus) to local level (e.g. buying a club's kit). The sport is seeking sponsors for junior squads, coaching films and leagues, and the marketing possibilities are immense. In 1981 I wrote, 'One feels that athletics is about to be transformed and its amateur myths dispelled. When this happens we may see stars like Ovett and Coe earning the kind of money that is now commonplace in golf or tennis. But television tends to flatter the sport, eliminating the tedious intervals between events and lack of facilities that make 'entertaining' business clients virtually impossible.'

Since then, much has happened: top athletes now earn sizeable sums[3] and the sports and marketing agency, Alan Pascoe Associates, has been signed up by the athletics governing bodies to market their televised events up to 1990.

Gymnastics is said to attract support worth £1 million a year, although sponsorship began in earnest only in the mid 1970s. The

British Amateur Gymnastics Association claims that more than four million people perform some form of gymnastics each day of the week and that all its events at Wembley Arena (seating capacity 50,000) are 'sell-outs'. Its eight television programmes each year are sold throughout the world and one event had an estimated audience of 200 million people. The Association is in the happy position of being able to decide that it has reached maximum exposure with its current television sponsored events and is seeking no more sponsors for these. It does sometimes turn down substantial sponsorship offers because either the product is 'wrong' for the sport or it considers that the sponsor is expecting too much from the event.

NOTES

1. Since the voluntary agreement to maintain sponsorship at the 1976/77 level, with allowance for inflation, the proportion of sports sponsorship in the hands of tobacco companies had fallen in 1987 to around seven per cent in the UK, according to the Economist Intelligence Unit. However, a survey among the European readers of *Time* showed that two tobacco groups were still among the eight companies most conspicuously linked in the public mind with sponsorship.

2. *Today* newspaper's abrupt cancellation of its Football League sponsorship reflected some understandable pique at rival sponsors being given such icing on the cake as the showpiece Centenary match at Wembley – 'a bit like Allders getting the Santa's Grotto concession', observed the *Guardian's* David Lacey.

3. Zola Budd, the South African-born athlete who qualified to run for Britain despite a continuing rumble of disapproval from many quarters, reputedly received £90,000 for racing against the American Mary Decker-Slaney after the 1984 Olympics. And sprinters Ben Johnson and Carl Lewis shared $500,000 for racing 100 metres at Zurich in the weeks before the 1988 Olympic Games.

CHAPTER 5

The sports supermarket

In Chapter 4 we looked at some of the more heavily sponsored sports that, because of their popularity, command the widest audiences and have the greatest publicity potential. They represent the highly competitive end of the market, but would-be sponsors have increasingly reappraised the value of entering what is already becoming a densely populated area in which it will be more and more difficult to make any impact. High-profile televised events no longer take all the cake as more people realise how local events or minority sports can fit into an imaginative marketing plan.

Outside the main league waits a whole range of sports which could grow in popularity as society reacts to changes in leisure time and attitudes towards mass entertainment as compared to participant activities. Let us look at these other opportunities and, for convenience, take them in alphabetical order.

American football

The three-year £250,000 Budweiser sponsorship of a new league helped focus attention on this stranger to the British scene whose introduction owes much to what some may think of as the Orwellian influence of television. The US National Football League decided, a few years ago, to expand overseas and saw England as a good place to start because the game was not entirely unknown there, as it was played at US air bases. Furthermore, there was this national game called soccer, which was administered by people who had no notion how to market the game and little idea of what would appeal to young boys in the 1980s. Soccer, they decided, as seen on British television, was two 45-minute slabs of boredom. They also argued that American football matches, despite the on-field mayhem, are, in fact, family occasions unplagued by the kind of scenes that occur on the soccer terraces from time to time.

British American Football Association, Suite 3, 212 Old Christchurch Road, Bournemouth, Dorset BH1 1PD.

Angling

Angling is probably the most popular British pastime after gardening. There are said to be 3.5 million British anglers with an additional 59,000 taking it up every year. Sponsorship has come from tobacco firms and tackle suppliers and probably totals about only £200,000 annually. This is surprising since anglers form such a large consumer audience and, when engaged in their hobby, should be reasonably receptive to advertising. The problem is that as a televised spectacle the sport is a producer's nightmare since the fish cannot be relied upon to take the bait on camera cue.

National Anglers' Council, 11 Cowgate, Peterborough PE1 1LZ. Tel: Peterborough (0733) 54084.

Archery

With only 17,000 active participants, archery has so far failed to tempt sponsors or television very much. Modern camera techniques should be able to make it visually stunning. Target archery is perhaps too slow and long-winded, – so is golf, of course – but it takes little imagination to foresee variations that could provide more excitement without going as far as William Tell. Field Archery, shot across country, is even more stimulating to watch. Locally, regionally or nationally, archery events can be sponsored for as little as £1,000.

Grand National Archery Society, 7th Street, National Agricultural Centre, Stoneleigh, Kenilworth, Warwickshire CV8 2LG. Tel: Coventry (0203) 696631.

Association football (see Chapter 4)

Women's football in England, run by the Women's Football Association, offers sponsorship at modest cost: £2,000–£3,000 for an international game, £6,000 for the WFA National Challenge Trophy Competition, and up to £1,000 for the All England Indoor Five-a-sides or under-16 events. Normal league matches played on park pitches each Sunday command small audiences and the highest attendance for a match played on a Football League ground was 5,471. The WFA has 235 clubs with a total playing strength of 6,000 (aged from 12 to 40). About another 150 clubs are found in Scotland, Wales and Northern Ireland.

Football Association Limited, 16 Lancaster Gate, London W2 3LW. Tel: 01-262 4542.

Women's Football Association, 11 Portsea Mews, Portsea Place, London W2 2BN. Tel: 01-402 9388.

Athletics (see Chapter 4)

The 1980s have seen marathon running turn into a mass-participation industry – 100,000 people apply for 23,000 places in the London Marathon which attracts sponsors such as Mars at £150,000. The number of full marathons has declined from the 1983 peak of 136 but sponsorship opportunities abound in the host of half- or mini-marathons, usually associated with raising money for charity.

Amateur Athletic Association, M. A. Farrell, Francis House, Francis Street, London SW1P 1DL. Tel: 01-828 9326.

Badminton

Badminton has an estimated 1.5 million players in the United Kingdom and attracts £400,000 worth of sponsorship. This varies from big international events in the £25,000-plus category to sponsoring local clubs. There are about 6,000 clubs and the growth of the sport is closely linked to the growth in the number of sports centres. Television is taking increasing interest and the sport should be looked at seriously by potential sponsors, especially those keen on family and school associations.

Badminton Association of England, 44–45 Palace Road, Bromley, Kent BR1 3JU. Tel: 01-464 0031.

Ballooning

The British Balloon and Airship Club is the governing body and has a membership of 2,000, including 350 registered pilots. While it has obvious promotion and advertising applications, ballooning remains a sponsorship 'outsider' with the occasional imaginative event giving it the glamour and media coverage that a sponsor may seek.

British Balloon and Airship Club, PO Box 1006, Birmingham B5 5RT.

Baseball

Baseball is chiefly of interest to firms with connections in Europe, especially the Netherlands, where coverage is good on radio and television. Britain has only about 1,000 registered players and even the biggest international fixture, Great Britain *v.* France, attracts a modest 1,000 gate. But 1986 may have been a turning point with Channel Four's coverage of the World Series and the sponsorship of the BBF by Scottish Amicable. Anyone who has seen top-class American baseball

in its own setting will need no convincing of the visual appeal of this most operatic of games and Channel Four is becoming an excellent evangelist – and interpreter – of such unfamiliar activities.
British Baseball Federation, 197 Newbridge Road, Hull, North Humberside HU9 2LR. Tel: Hull (0482) 76169.

Basketball

Basketball is played by 500,000 people in the UK, and the English Basketball Association estimates the number of spectators at the same figure. The injection of sponsorship, now running at around £500,000 per year, has enabled the competitions and teams to develop, and major events are now covered regularly by national television.

Basketball is one sport that has taken a serious look at sponsorship and its role, and can offer a comprehensive shopping list that includes events with extensive television coverage (£50,000–£150,000), involvement with national teams (£30,000), coaching and development programmes (£15,000) or individual club sponsorships (£5,000–£50,000).
English Basketball Association, Calomax House, Lupton Avenue, Leeds LS9 7EE. Tel: Leeds (0532) 496044.

Billiards and snooker

Estimates of participants vary between 6 million and 8 million, and television has revived and enhanced interest in snooker. Among the best-known sponsorships is the Embassy World Professional Snooker Championship, where the prize fund is above £100,000. The company also has to bear promotional and hidden costs. Other sponsors may have been put off by the sport's overexposure. However, sponsorship of amateur snooker and the more elegant game of billiards remains comparatively unexplored. The Billiards and Snooker Foundation is responsible for a national coaching scheme to train under-18s in the basic techniques, and many boys and girls are given tuition each year.
Billiards and Snooker Control Council, Coronet House, Queen Street, Leeds LS1 2TN. Tel: Leeds (0532) 440586.

Bobsleigh

Bobsleigh has had little sponsorship although it does receive some television coverage. The British Bobsleigh Olympic team is closely followed on television and in the press. The sport is expensive and exclusive: the British Bobsleigh Association has 140 members, only 40 of whom are active. It can clearly offer opportunities for the right sponsor but needs careful study and planning.

British Bobsleigh Association, 50 Sulivan Street, London SW6 3DX. Tel: 01-736 9795.

Bowls

Bowls is said to be second only to angling among participant sports and it has the 'mini-green' quality of being a television natural – like snooker, lawn tennis and golf. Because of the number of different official organisations involved, would-be sponsors have to do their homework carefully – for instance, flat green, crown green, indoor and federation bowling each has its own administration. With a playing population of half a million and a potential television audience at least as large as those attracted by snooker and darts, bowls must have almost the greatest potential of all the less obvious sports. Much depends upon the attitudes of the governing bodies and whether or not their quite understandable fears of being taken over can be allayed. Indoor bowls offers attractive possibilities. In England, for example, 70,000 people play at 200 stadia, many of which are part of sports complexes, the rest being purpose-built and privately run. National championships are beginning to attract new sponsors and the outlook is bright, with 'plums' such as the Embassy World Indoor event offering a £16,000 top prize.

English Bowling Association, 2a Iddesleigh Road, Bournemouth BH3 7JR. Tel: Bournemouth (0202) 22233.

Boxing

This is regarded as a dangerous sport (although, statistically, it is probably less so than soccer) and is therefore unattractive to many sponsors. I do not refer here to professional boxing tournaments, which are run by licensed promoters who receive the profits and have no need for sponsors, even though sponsors are now often on the scene at televised events. Individual professional boxers have, however, received sponsorship, for example DAF Trucks' connection with Alan Minter (£35,000) and Whyte & Mackay's support for Maurice Hope and Jim Watts. Amateur boxing, sponsored by George Wimpey PLC since 1980, has 30,000 participants, and sponsorship scope ranges from £100 to sponsor a single contest to £8,000 for a full tournament. It is still an excellent spectator sport with attendances of between 1,000 and 11,000.

Amateur Boxing Association, Francis House, Francis Street, London SW1P 1DE. Tel: 01-828 8571.

Bridge

Although not officially recognised as a sport, tournament bridge deserves a sponsor's attention. If one includes the home-based rubber bridge enthusiasts, Britain probably claims more than two million players, yet, says the English Bridge Union, 'No major advertiser has really got down to testing the benefits which this market might hold for him.' Competition bridge is governed by the EBU whose 27,000 members have the sex, socio-economic and age profiles shown in Table 5.1.

Table 5.1 Sex, socio-economic and age profiles of EBU members

	Male: 57%		Female: 43%	
AB: 78%		C1: 19%		Others: 3%
	Total (%)	Male (%)	Female (%)	
Over 65	9	5	17	
Over 45	38	31	46	
Over 25	36	43	29	
Under 25	17	21	8	

Consider that the 2 million players have a significant interest in tobacco, food and drink, travel and tourism, cars, computers, furniture, domestic appliances, investment, banking and insurance. Consider also that, with increased leisure time, more and more people will learn to play bridge, that it is being taught in evening institutes and clubs throughout the country and even in sixth forms at school, and that regular articles appear on the game in six national daily newspapers, four Sunday newspapers and at least four up-market weekly magazines. Bridge is one of the few remaining sponsorship fields that offers cost-effective sponsorship and that has so far remained relatively untapped. Many companies have nibbled at the bait, but none has so far established a dominant role.

English Bridge Union, Broadfields, Bicester Road, Aylesbury, Buckinghamshire HP19 3BG. Tel: Aylesbury (0296) 394 414.

Canoeing
Canoeing is in the process of changing from a major-minor sport to a minor-major sport. The British Canoe Union official who told me this also pointed out that, each year in Britain, a million people get into canoes, but the number who do so through the 500 official clubs is nearer 250,000.

The sport has a healthy image, a spice of risk and is extremely watchable. Potential audiences for rough-water canoeing are enormous and sponsorship is needed at all levels – regional, national and international – in all types of competition. The cost varies, starting at around £2,000 for a two-day national youth championship to the £2.25 million National Canoeing Centre with its artificial slalom and white-water course.

British Canoe Union, 45 High Street, Addlestone, Weybridge, Surrey KT15 1JV. Tel: Weybridge (0932) 841341.

Chess

Chess has possibilities similar to those of bridge, and annual sponsorship has increased to more than £200,000, with finance and computer companies prominent. Lloyds Bank is probably the best known sponsor of chess at all levels with special interest in junior and women's chess (eg the Lloyds Bank Lady Masters, a somewhat ambiguous title which may have alienated feminist account holders). The bank identifies chess as the tenth most popular participation sport in the 15–19 age group and therefore a cost-effective way of reaching this important audience.

British Chess Federation, 4 The Close, Norwich NR1 4DH. Tel: Norwich (0603) 612678.

Clay pigeon shooting

Clay pigeon shooting did not attract the sponsorship that might have been expected after its successful year in 1979, when British shooters brought home 30 medals, including ten golds, from major international events abroad. It would appear to be a natural and photogenic vehicle for advertising a whole range of products and would not bring sponsoring companies into conflict with anti-bloodsport activists. In recent years it has established a toehold in television. It is one of the growth sports and is used by companies to give employees a day out. Many shooting grounds now run such company days, providing tuition, lunch and shooting.

Clay Pigeon Shooting Association, 107 Epping New Road, Buckhurst Hill, Essex IG9 5TQ. Tel: 01-505 6221.

Cricket (see Chapter 4)

MCC, Test and County Cricket Board, Lord's, St John's Wood, London NW8. Tel: 01-289 1615.

Croquet

Memories of garden croquet and a long-ago lesson from ex-World

Champion Miss D. D. Steel – then a sprightly septuagenarian – suggest to the writer that croquet, the gentle, artful, if not to say spiteful, game, has enormous television potential. My hope that it remain undiscovered (and unspoiled) by sponsorship is doomed, it seems. Croquet is now one of the world's fastest growing sports with up to 400,000 players, 145 clubs and 130 tournaments each year in Britain. Granada Television has started to show the game (1987/8) which is now attracting ever-younger players – the 1987 Open winner was 21-year-old Mark Avery and among the 12 best players competing for the President's Cup were two under-18s. Sponsorship income to the CA is around £50,000 but things could alter in this rapidly changing sport.

Croquet Association, Hurlingham Club, Ranelagh Gardens, London SW6 3PR. Tel: 01-736 3148.

Cycling (see also Chapter 4)

There are around 15 million cycles owned in Britain and annual sales now top two million. All age groups (from 9 to 90 claims the BCF) relate to this most accessible pastime and sponsorship opportunities are numerous. The Milk Race is now in its 30th year of sponsorship by the National Dairy Council, the longest involvement of any, and its £400,000 budget puts it at least in sight of the £1-million Tour de France. Cycling, therefore, is efficiently marketed and all kinds of competitions, races, track events, etc., are available for sponsorship in the £1,000–£7,500 range. Sponsoring British teams gets the company name and logo on tracksuits, leisure and race clothing, and team support vehicles. The cost begins at around £4,000 and can rise to the £40,000 asked for supporting the 1988 Olympics challenge in South Korea.

British Cycling Federation, 16 Upper Woburn Place, London WC1H 0QE. Tel: 01-387 9320.

Darts

As recently as 1977, darts was referred to as a pub sport, and therefore as a sponsorship vehicle appropriate only for companies such as breweries, tobacco companies and manufacturers of darts equipment.

Much has happened since then, with the sport receiving maximum television exposure while retaining its essentially participant nature. Estimates of the number of people playing competitively and socially (including presumably, Auntie Eva having her annual fling at double top over Christmas) are seven million, and leisure and holiday groups,

bookmakers and motor companies are now joining the sponsors, who between them spend more than £500,000, seeking access to this huge audience.
British Darts Organisation, 2 Pages Lane, Muswell Hill, London N10 1PS. Tel: 01-883 5544.

Equestrian events (see Chapter 4)

British Equestrian Promotions Ltd, 35 Belgrave Square, London SW1X 8QB. Tel: 01-235 6472.

Fencing

Fencing is a participant sport with approximately 15,000 actively taking part. It has few spectators and little television coverage. Martini & Rossi, National Westminster, Diners Club and Wilkinson Sword have been sponsors, and wider sponsorship is always being sought by the Amateur Fencing Association. Many years ago, Charles de Beaumont, doyen of British fencers, told me that fencing, because of its wide appeal to both sexes and its benefits as a form of year-round exercise, could well enjoy a dramatic expansion. So far his hopes have not been fulfilled, partly because television has yet to use its full technical wizardry (action replays, slow motion, etc.) to extract the best of this quicksilver sport for mass audience appreciation. The comparatively modest – up to £5,000 – cost is worth looking at.
Amateur Fencing Association, De Beaumont Centre, 83 Perham Road, London W14 9SP. Tel: 01-385 7442.

Gliding

A participant sport with about 10,500 devotees, gliding attracts few spectators because the interesting bits take place out of sight. Therefore sponsorship has been sparse and intermittent, although Allied Breweries' £10,000 sponsorship of the National Glider Championship enabled the sport to improve press facilities, thus drawing more coverage and, of course, making sponsorship more attractive. Marconi (now GEC Avionics) is one of the latest sponsors and there appears to be a good match of sport and product.
British Gliding Association Limited, Kimberley House, Vaughan Way, Leicester LE1 4SG. Tel: Leicester (0533) 51051.

Golf (see Chapter 4)

Royal and Ancient Golf Club, St Andrews, Fife, Scotland. Tel: St Andrews (0334) 72112.

Greyhound racing

Greyhound racing has largely succeeded in losing its 'cloth cap' image and now has a considerable following among young people and about £500,000 worth of sponsorship is provided each year. About the same amount is raised each year by co-sponsorship between the racing operators and major charities.

Greyhound Racing Association Limited, White City Stadium, London W12. Tel: 01-743 5544.

Gymnastics (see Chapter 4)

British Amateur Gymnastics Association, Ford Hall, Lilleshall National Sports Centre, near Newport, Shropshire TF10 9NB. Tel: Newport (0952) 607137.

Sponsorship inquiries to: Tony Murdock, 2 Buckingham Avenue East, Slough, Berkshire SL1 3DZ. Tel: Slough (0753) 34171/71422.

Handball

Handball has yet to make an impact in Britain, although there is a national league and more schools are taking it up. Olympic Games' coverage has helped to explain the game's simple and popular appeal – it is all about scoring goals, exciting to watch, simple to learn and involves running, catching, throwing and jumping. It is exceptionally popular in Germany and Scandinavia, even vying with soccer. It is a fine media sport if handled properly and attracts big audiences in Europe. The sport needs help with marketing, through sponsorship, although Bells Whisky have made a start.

British Handball Association, 68 Penryn Avenue, Fishermead, Milton Keynes, Buckinghamshire. Tel: Milton Keynes (0908) 678339.

Hang gliding

Offering an obvious medium for advertising, hang gliding could well attract sponsorship interest. The British Hang Gliding Association has 4,000 members and many thousands more attend training schools. While it is a big crowd-puller, it is difficult to assess hang gliding's spectator level.

Individuals are sponsored by firms who buy a glider and sail which advertises a product, and there is potential for sponsoring clubs and teams in international competitions. It lends itself superbly to televising, and small-time sponsorship would cost around £1,000. Clubs always need help to send teams overseas. The British team has had many successes and the BHGA can lay on a specific public event for an interested sponsor (cost from about £10,000).

British Hang Gliding Association, 167A Cheddon Road, Taunton, Somerset TA2 7AH. Tel: Taunton (0823) 88140.

Hockey (field)

Hockey is currently enjoying a boom as a result of the bronze medal won by the Great Britain men's team in the 1984 Los Angeles Olympics and the silver medal won by the England men at the 1986 World Cup in London. These successes and the major television coverage have boosted participation in the game and attracted new sponsorship. The men's World Cup in 1986 attracted more than 92,000 spectators over the 12-day period, and on three of the days there was a capacity crowd of 12,000. Chief sponsors are Lada Cars, (£420,000) with a three-year agreement to sponsor an annual four-nations men's tournament and the British Cities Indoor Championship. The Royal Bank of Scotland sponsors the Hockey Association's Indoor Club Championship and other sponsors include Puma, which provides all the playing equipment to both Great Britain and England men, Slazengers, National Westminster Bank, Nationwide Anglia Building Society, Dexters Sports Drinks, Kookaburra Balls, Chantrey Wood King and Readersport. The Great Britain men's hockey squad is also sponsored by Minet Holdings PLC.

The All England Women's Hockey Association is attracting more sponsorship and is currently supported by Tipp-Ex, which sponsors the Wembley International; the National Westminster Bank, which supports the County Championship and Under-21 Territorial Tournament and Barclays Bank.

Both Associations are still seeking sponsorship support for a wide range of domestic and international matches and championships, indoor and outdoor.

Stephen Baines, Chief Executive, The Hockey Association, 16 Northdown Street, London N1 9BG. Tel: 01-837 8878.

Teresa Morris, Secretary, All England Women's Hockey Association, Third Floor, Argyle House, 29–31 Euston Road, London NW1 2SD. Tel: 01-278 6340.

Hockey (ice)

After being moribund for some years, this sport has revived dramatically recently with a flush of new rinks and the three-division Senior League attracted a £500,000 sponsor by Heineken (over two years). Premier division teams also attract individual sponsorships and Norwich Union took on the Cup event for £50,000 (1985–88).

British Ice Hockey Association, 40 Hambledon Road, Boscombe East, Bournemouth BH7 6PQ. Tel: Bournemouth (0202) 432583.

Hockey (roller)

Roller hockey is a Cinderella sport that actually had its origins at about the turn of the century and has been administered since 1913 by the National Roller Hockey Association. Senior and junior leagues are organised as well as county championships, and there are European and World Championships at which England was supreme between the two World Wars. The sport depends upon a resurgence in the popularity of roller skating and an increase in the number of rinks, such as one observes in Canada. Perhaps the growth of new sports centres will provide the necessary spur.

National Roller Hockey Association of Great Britain, 22 Winterborne Avenue, Orpington, Kent BR6 9RH. Tel: Orpington (0689) 51514.

Lacrosse

Lacrosse has developed rapidly in the last few years and is played throughout the country by schools, colleges and clubs. Pop-lacrosse is being promoted, especially in inner city areas, as the flexible introduction to the full field game of both men's and women's lacrosse. It is estimated that 20,000 people have been introduced to the game through pop-lacrosse and that about 40,000 girls and women, and 15,000 boys and men, now play field lacrosse.

Leagues and inter-club fixtures occupy most of the calendar, with county, territorial and international matches being the highlights of the season. Most internationals attract a few thousand spectators, especially the World Cups which are held every four years.

All England Women's Lacrosse Association, Francis House, Francis Street, London SW1P 1DE. Tel: 01-931 8899.

English Lacrosse Union, Rycroft Mills, Ashton-under-Lyne, Lancashire OL7 0DB. Tel: 061-339 7508.

Land yachting

Land yachting is almost virgin soil for sponsors. Today's sleek and colourful yachts have come a long way from the crude and relatively slow craft of the past and can demonstrate close racing speeds in excess of 80 m.p.h. Even the class V yachts, throwing up vast clouds of spray and with rarely more than two of the three wheels on the ground, regularly exceed 60 m.p.h. It has not yet become a spectator sport, but Britain has produced many world champions of both sexes.

The governing body actively promotes the sport and receives

media interest, often for special projects such as encouraging the handicapped or juniors. These and other events, such as the launch of a new club, are supported by top sailors drawn from the British team.

The British Federation of Sand and Land Yacht Clubs, 23 Piper Drive, Long Whatton, Loughborough, Leicestershire LE12 5DJ. Tel: Loughborough (0509) 842292.

Lawn tennis (see Chapter 4)

Lawn Tennis Association, The Queens Club, West Kensington, London W14 9EG. Tel: 01-385 2366.

Motor racing (see Chapter 4)

RAC Motor Sports Association, 31 Belgrave Square, London SW1X 8QH. Tel: 01-235 8601.

Netball

Netball is an exciting game dominated by women, which requires teamwork, fitness and skill. The sport has grown in prominence in recent years and the governing body is determined to increase its level of exposure. Club membership numbers are increasing rapidly and England is currently ranked fourth in the world. Sponsorship opportunities exist within every level of competition and within development projects. Depending upon the television coverage, sponsoring an international match can cost between £5,000 and £15,000 and a successor is needed to National Westminster who contributed more than £100,000 over seven years to training and coaching.

The All England Netball Association Ltd, Francis House, Francis Street, London SW1P 1DE. Tel: 01-828 2176.

Orienteering

Although probably not the most stimulating spectator sport, orienteering does attract some sponsorship and more than 200,000 people take part every year. The British Orienteering Federation claims it is a family sport which attracts participants from a wide age range – 10-year-olds to over-65s. More than 1,250 events take place each year in all parts of the country and orienteers travel extensively. Present sponsors are TSB Trust Company (major events, rankings list, publicity literature and badge award scheme); The Paper Sack Information Bureau (major international event) and Silva UK Ltd (junior squad).

The sport is increasingly being taken up as a community recreation activity and there are considerable developments with schools. This,

combined with the unique nature of the sport, gives sponsorship opportunities with excellent local publicity throughout the country. The national championships would cost a sponsor around £5,000.
The British Orienteering Federation, Riversdale, Dale Road North, Darley Dale, Matlock, Derbyshire DE4 2HX. Tel: Matlock (0629) 734042.

Parachuting

Parachuting, or skydiving, attracts about 45,000 participants and provides good spectator displays for the family when conditions are right. During the last few years, many national teams have been backed by major manufacturing companies, e.g. USA – Budweiser, France – Coca Cola and now TAG-Heuer. The British Parachute Association says that sponsorship for teams taking part in the world championships is being actively sought. In the last ten years, the British teams have won one gold, one silver and have been placed fourth on two occasions in the different disciplines competed for each year. It can cost the Association around £12,000 to stage the national championships, and in the region of £20,000 to enter the British teams in a world championship.
British Parachute Association, Wharf Way, Glen Parva, Leicester LE2 9TF. Tel: Leicester (0533) 785271.

Polo

Polo's exclusive, up-market image obviously limits its appeal, and it can scarcely be described as a major participant sport. It does attract several thousand spectators to big events and there is scope for using it as an entertainment vehicle through tournament marquees and so on. It has obvious associations with luxury goods and sponsors have included Cartier, Davidoff and Pimms. Sponsoring a high-grade team for a season, with perhaps exclusive use of a tournament included, would cost around £100,000.
Hurlingham Polo Association, Pephurst Farm, Loxwood, Billingshurst, West Sussex RH14 0RW. Tel: Loxwood (0403) 752738.

Powerboat racing

This is the marine version of motor racing and, being similarly expensive, requires heavy sponsorship. It makes good television viewing with a season of international and national races. Sponsors have included tobacco and drinks companies and the press.
Royal Yachting Association, RYA House, Romsey Road, Eastleigh, Hampshire SO5 4YA. Tel: Eastleigh (0703) 629962.

Roller hockey (see Hockey (roller))

Rowing

Several hundred rowing regattas each year, ranging from Henley Royal Regatta, the world's most prestigious rowing event, to town and city events, involve some 20,000 oarsmen/oarswomen and junior competitors throughout the country. Most press coverage is local, with national coverage being mainly restricted to the up-market dailies. There is scope for sponsorship at national championships and other major events such as the National Schools Regatta and Nottinghamshire International Regatta and in national squad and Olympic team training. Television coverage achieved recently was of the highest quality and the sport is trying to exploit its clean-cut and wholesome image to attract more. The annual University Boat Race on the Thames is exceptional and has been sponsored by Ladbrokes (at £60,000).

Amateur Rowing Association, 6 Lower Mall, London W6 9DJ. Tel: 01-748 3632/2.

Rugby Union

Rugby Union 'pussy-footed' with sponsorship for 10 or 15 years and, at local club level, welcomed unobtrusive help from breweries. The association with John Player has, however, provided an ironic link with its 'untouchable' cousin, Rugby League, since the 'John Player Cup' is now the national club competition for both codes. The floodgates were opened and a variety of companies like Thorn EMI, Courage, Schweppes, Bowrings and Stewart Wrightson (now Willis Faber) have supported the game to something like £1 million a year. This does not include individual club deals. The change in attitude was underlined in 1985 when the RFU appointed a marketing manager and the long-awaited 15-a-side world championship was born in 1987.

Rugby League is confined chiefly to the north of England but has overseas links that almost parallel those of Rugby Union. It, too, claims sponsorship at the £1 million a year level with Stone's Bitter taking over the league championship from Slalom Lager.

Rugby Football Union, Whitton Road, Twickenham, Middlesex TW2 7RQ. Tel: 01-892 8161.

Rugby Football League, 180 Chapeltown Road, Leeds LS7 4HT. Tel: Leeds (0532) 624637.

Sailing

Sailing offers a bewildering variety of sponsorship opportunities, ranging from small club events to round-the-world ventures and extravagant prestige events such as the America's Cup. Because of its diversification it will always be a difficult area for would-be sponsors, and its very nature tends to foster enthusiasm at the expense of objectivity. However, the healthy image of boat and sea, wind and weather will doubtless continue to prove irresistible.

Royal Yachting Association, RYA House, Romsey Road, Eastleigh, Hampshire SO5 4YA. Tel: Eastleigh (0703) 629962.

Shooting

This sport is basically for participants and may seem to have little obvious appeal for sponsors not associated with weapon or ammunition manufacture. Nevertheless, shooting in all its forms is the second most popular participatory sport in the country, and the National Rifle Association says some 50,000 people shoot in the United Kingdom and about 3,000 take part in events at Bisley, the shooting centre of Great Britain. The NRA receives some sponsorship with firms presenting prizes of up to £700, but there is scope for further sponsorship of major competitions in the Association's annual meeting which are progressively receiving more publicity and attracting increased participation from home and overseas and larger crowds.

National Rifle Association, Bisley Camp, Brookwood, Woking, Surrey GU24 0PB. Tel: Brookwood (048 67) 2213/4 and 5556.

Skiing

With its obvious television appeal, skiing is a growth area for sponsors, and the British Ski Federation reports that a million Britons ski each year. Internationally, a variety of companies have had some involvement, and the choice ranges from minor races on artificial slopes (cost £5,000) to sponsoring teams in major European events (cost £50,000–£100,000).

The British Ski Federation organises the British Alpine senior, junior and children's Ski Championships, the British Nordic Cross-country and Biathlon Championships and other British national events on snow, plastic and grass. Many of these events are sponsored but opportunities occur from time to time. The Federation also organises the training and racing of a 'development squad' of six boys and six girls for Alpine, four in the Nordic team and seven in the Biathlon team (both men only). The Alpine team now has a £500,000 sponsorship by Drambuie over three years.

Other Olympic winter sports, such as **skating**, receive television coverage and a limited amount of sponsorship.

British Ski Federation, 118 Eaton Square, London SW1W 9AF. Tel: 01-235 8227/8.

National Skating Association of Great Britain, 117 Charterhouse Street, London EC1M 6AT. Tel: 01-253 3824/5.

Squash

Squash has been 'rapidly expanding' for many years, but television has only recently started to follow its fortunes in a major way. The game was said to be too fast for the camera and the usual squash court was not a very salubrious place. Technical breakthroughs have improved viewing possibilities with the 'perspex' court allowing the audience to see in through all walls whilst the players cannot see out. Alongside this innovation was the development of the 'televisual' ball whose flight the television cameras could pick up more readily. Played on a green painted floor instead of the customary natural wood, the game has taken an upward turn in spectator capabilities and an all-time record of 3,526 went to the Royal Albert Hall to watch the final of the 1988 World Championships.

Some three million participants in Britain play squash on conventional courts and the game is highly popular. Most squash players are in the 15–34 age group; two thirds are men, one third women. Current sponsors include ICI, American Express, InterCity and Hi-Tec Sports, all with different reasons for involvement, and present sponsorship figures are up to £200,000 for any one sponsorship. Opportunities are often available or can be tailored to suit the needs of potential sponsors.

Squash Rackets Association, Francis House, Francis Street, London SW1P 1DE. Tel: 01-828 3064.

Surfing

This sport attracts between 8,000 and 10,000 participants throughout Britain. Major championships draw up to 100,000 spectators over a weekend. The sport is spectacular and makes excellent television. Sponsorship is always needed: a championship like the European requires a budget of around £20,000, but smaller championships, such as the English, Welsh and Great Britain, can be sponsored for up to £5,000.

British Surfing Association, 30 Parkstone Road, Poole, Dorset. Tel: Poole (0202) 381310.

Swimming

An obvious major participant sport, swimming is popular with sponsors at various levels. Major championships attract television coverage, the sport has associations with young people, and there is scope for grass-roots help in training, tuition, coaching and the supporting spin-offs, such as wall charts and other educational aids in addition to tracksuits, swimwear, etc. Banks, newspapers, food manufacturers and, of course, makers of swimming pools are among those who have sponsored the sport, while tobacco companies and brewers have not been encouraged because of the large numbers of young participants.

New sponsors who feel that the sport now offers little scope might consult the British Long-distance Swimming Association which is seeking commercial support. It arranges a variety of events from three-mile 'sprints' to the Loch Lomond championship at 24 miles, or the spectacular 'Windermere 25-kilometre International', at which the world's best amateur long-distance swimmers represent their countries for the team award.

Amateur Swimming Association, Harold Fern House, Derby Square, Loughborough, Leicestershire LE11 0AC. Tel: Loughborough (0509) 230431.
British Long-distance Swimming Association, 40 Brook Drive, Great Sankey, nr Warrington, Cheshire WA5 1RY. Tel: Penketh (092 572) 6550.

Table tennis

Table tennis is one of the most popular sports with over two million participants in the UK. It has now successfully bridged the gap between amateur playing and a successfully sponsored professional circuit. Sponsorship of table tennis commenced in 1977; the world championships in Birmingham, supported by Norwich Union, benefited from 35 hours of television coverage. Norwich Union supported table tennis for many years but after its withdrawal, sponsorship was limited until the Leeds Permanent Building Society announced in 1987 a three-year package of sponsorship for the sport, totalling over £500,000. This package ranges from support at the junior and grass-roots level, through the Leeds British League to the high-profile Leeds Euro-Asia and Leeds English Open Championships. The sport is now receiving wide coverage on Channel Four and BBC 1 and many observers believe it is as potentially appealing to the television viewer as darts, snooker and bowls.

English Table Tennis Association, 21 Claremont, Hastings, East Sussex TN34 1HA. Tel: Hastings (0424) 433522.

Tennis (real) and rackets

These sports have a limited appeal but a loyal and expanding following. The small prospect of television coverage has not deterred the occasional sponsor who sees these games reaching a small but highly selective audience.

Tennis and Rackets Association, The Queen's Club, Palliser Road, London W14 9EQ. Tel: 01-381 4746.

Volleyball

Volleyball is one of those sports (30,000 players) that is gaining wide popularity and by 1990 aims to be the fifth major (in terms of the number of competitors) team sport in Britain. It is an Olympic event and has world and international championships. Sponsorship is modest despite increasing television coverage on Channel Four and BBC, although the Royal Bank of Scotland moved in to sponsor the major English league and cup events. International tournaments are among the many sponsorship opportunities still available.

English Volleyball Association, 13 Rectory Road, West Bridgford, Nottingham NG2 6EP. Tel: Nottingham (0602) 816324.

Water skiing

With over 120,000 participants, water skiing is a growing participant and spectator sport offering visibility to sponsors. Opportunities are available for sponsorship from local to international level.

The sport has received excellent television coverage of its major events which have been sponsored by companies seeking a vehicle that has excitement, glamour and adventure for product identification.

British Water Ski Federation, 390 City Road, London EC1V 2QA. Tel: 01-833 2855/6.

Weightlifting

The British Amateur Weight Lifters Association is seeking sponsors in various areas of responsibility. These include international matches, training sessions for the national squad (£8,000 a year), coaching schemes (about £5,000), schoolboy championships (a national level of 300 boys would cost £1,000 in publicity and backing), and aids such as wall charts showing exercises for weight training, etc.

British Amateur Weight Lifters Association Limited, 3 Iffley Turn, Oxford OX4 4DU. Tel: Oxford (0865) 778319.

Wrestling

The amateur sport of wrestling seeks sponsors for four or five tournaments each year and, with ten weight categories, sponsorship could be provided by several sponsors or by a single backer.

English Olympic Wrestling Association, 16 Choir Street, Salford, Manchester M7 9ZD. Tel: Manchester (061) 832 9209.

CHAPTER 6

The arts bazaar

The arts offer opportunities for sponsorship that differ from those available in sport and perhaps demand a more delicate and subtle approach. Some years ago, when I was addressing a conference in London, I said there might come a day when arts organisations would find themselves in the enviable position of Gaiety Girls. Instead of having to go to industry with their begging bowls, they might find themselves to be highly prized, in short supply and pursued by crowds of stage-door Johnnies. Hard-pressed treasurers may consider such thinking wishful and in reality any organisation can only offer a reasonable return on investment to a limited number of sponsors. Thus, paradoxically, the very speed of business sponsorship's advance could create its own problems, since, inevitably, the supply of desirable projects will not keep pace with the demand.

Most London orchestras even now have more than four or five sponsors, which enables them to offer each one seven or eight concerts in a full season, if required. Overseas or provincial tours are available to such long-standing supporters, but it is significant that foreign companies are beginning to seek associations with prestigious British culture. Britain is to the performing arts what Saudi Arabia is to the world's energy resources, and the only surprise is that it has taken so long for foreign entrepreneurs to start drilling.

The arts have become the fastest-growing area in British sponsorship, with an annual income approaching £30 million. In November 1980 Mr Norman St John-Stevas, the then Arts Minister, predicted that support would treble within two years. Many thought he was being fanciful but support for the arts has consistently outpaced the overall sponsorship rate.

The Economist Intelligence Unit's two suggested reasons for this are familiar ones: the increasing emphasis on social responsibility, and the fact that it is still possible to get a satisfactory deal at lower cost in the arts. That is why the financial pages of national newspapers continue to marvel that business sponsorship of the arts is bravely riding out the recession and pumping money into music, drama, ballet and other activities while turnover and profits are falling. On the arts pages the writers will be pointing out that, whatever the sum spent on sponsorship, it is negligible in relation to overall profits.

For potential sponsors, the arts bazaar offers a bewildering variety of glamorous goods, from opera and ballet, to theatre, films, festivals, exhibitions, poetry. Some years ago, businessmen entered this emporium with diffidence, like the nervous nouveau stepping inside Aspreys of Old Bond Street, cowed by the apparent air of sophistication and scared of making a fool of himself. In the early days some hasty and ill-considered decisions were taken. Now the principle of *quid pro quo* is established and there is no excuse for repeating old blunders.

Understandably, music is the most popular of the arts among sponsors; it can be enjoyed in so many different ways and it reaches an infinite variety of people both at home and abroad, and the fact that it raises no language barriers makes it of special interest to international companies. Sponsors find music easy to buy, they know what they are getting and can match it exactly to their target audience. From an artistic viewpoint, this may not be entirely satisfactory. It means that the experimental, the new, the innovative and the risky are less likely to attract sponsorship than the familiar safe production; this became known as 'the Mozart factor'.

There are those who will argue that the funding of 'new' music should be left to the Arts Council, but I believe that arts organisers must take up the challenge of persuading business sponsors that, ultimately, they will gain as much prestige, if not more, from supporting the spirit of adventure in the arts. Tomorrow's consumers, the younger generation, have their own attitude to life and leisure that neither arts organisers nor businessmen have really begun to understand. To take one small example, what efforts have been made by Establishment music administrators to comprehend the enormous appeal for most youngsters of modern music involving synthesised sound?

One-off concerts are of limited benefit to the sponsor unless there is a specific occasion or an anniversary, but supporting an orchestra can be the most rewarding and durable of music sponsorships. Orchestral music is an extensive and widely popular form of expression and commands the largest music audiences. Certainly, when Eric Bravington, then approaching his twentieth year as Managing Director of the London Philharmonic Orchestra, first negotiated with me in the early 1970s, we did not realise how worthwhile Commercial Union's involvement would become and how lasting personal relationships between the two organisations would help draw them together.

A symphony orchestra unites the best of music and the best of musicians. The LPO, for instance, has performers like Nick Busch, a Kevin Keegan among horn players, and Gordon Hunt, prince among oboe players, and many more who, as individuals, are acclaimed by their peers. Together they blend their identities into one distinctive unity, and the style and character of an orchestra is uniquely its own and jealously preserved. To maintain this blend, orchestral players have to become members of a team playing together constantly. This is expensive and demands long-term financial security, yet orchestras are seriously threatened by financial problems.

Not untypical is the London Philharmonic Orchestra which has to perform the difficult, almost impossible, task of reconciling social contrasts, equal pay for women, human rights, racial or religious prejudices and worker participation at Board level. The Orchestra, by its Articles and because of its charitable status, is forbidden to distribute profits to its shareholders, and thus all but a small cash reserve is used to support this, one of the world's great symphony orchestras.

In Britain, where central and local government subsidies of principal orchestras run at about one-tenth those given to Continental orchestras, finance naturally plays a major part. Within a total present-day budget of around £2.5 million, the LPO Board must decide, with the guidance of its Managing Director (now John Willan), a list of priorities, and this is where this Company's unique position becomes apparent.

The LPO is governed by a Board of ten directors, seven being playing members elected from and by the shareholders at the annual general meeting. Directors stand down from the Board in rotation, usually after two to three years when they may retire or stand for re-election. Company shareholders are limited to playing members of the Orchestra. Each member may hold one nominal share for which he or she pays £1 three months after being accepted as a full member. On leaving the Orchestra, he or she automatically surrenders the share for the same sum of £1. The total share capital is £200.

The Board of Directors includes two non-executive directors and the Managing Director. Together, the Chairman, the Managing Director and their colleagues on the Board are responsible for every aspect of the Company's progress, both artistic and financial.

Chief priority is the Orchestra's artistic prowess, which, of course, governs its whole success. Each performance is given the maximum rehearsal time, and arrangements with leading international conductors for their exclusive services in the United Kingdom give the London Philharmonic a sure basis for the highest artistic standards. The programmes, again all chosen by the LPO's own management in consultation with the conductors it engages, must cover a repertoire that both appeals to as many people as possible and creates artistic interest for the players. To cover these aspects, a considerable part of the budget must be set aside.

Having appointed a small administrative staff of approximately 17 at rates that, while now more realistic than in the past, are still not abreast of commercial rates, the Board must also decide the Orchestra's salaries. Because of the small subsidy, there is no formal contract between the Orchestra's shareholding members and the Board; instead, everyone is on a fee-earning basis. There are fee structures for each of the types of appearance given by the Orchestra: concerts and rehearsals, children's concerts, recordings, television and radio sessions, opera performances and their attendant rehearsals, and, of course, foreign tours.

In deciding what rates should apply, the Board must consider: (a) the expected annual subsidy from the Arts Council of Great Britain; (b) fees for performances on recordings, television, radio, opera and foreign tours; (c) box-office return from tickets and programmes; (d) possible help from industry by sponsorship, buying advertising space in LPO programmes, and the sale of a full season's tickets for Royal Festival Hall concerts through the Orchestra's Corporate Membership scheme. When decided on, the rates, which must not be less than the minimum declared by the Musicians' Union, are based on four main levels: principal player, second principal, sub-principal, and rank and file. These terms show that the four distinct rates depend on the responsibility of the position occupied by each member.

Based on the above factors, a sensible and defensible structure is formed, and revised from time to time, depending on the state of the Company's progress and its small reserves. After settling this matter the Board:

(i)   makes some provision for holidays with pay, an arrangement that only became possible a few years ago;
(ii) allows for a small amount of sick benefit, although this is minimal compared with that received in most other jobs;
(iii) provides a pension scheme which will need rapid improvement to meet present-day needs.

Balancing the Company's budget is made possible by the members' spirit and understanding in determining their conditions of employment on a fee-earning basis. The management must ensure that the programme of concerts, recordings, etc., produces a work schedule that retains the services of all the players and it must seek financial support for such an operation by:

(1) negotiating with government bodies and industry;
(2) deciding on ticket pricing and programme policies that will attract maximum success at the box-office; and
(3) ensuring that the Orchestra's standards of performance attract the world's leading recording companies to offer continuing engagements.

The Orchestra's future would be bleak indeed if it depended solely on a government subsidy of about one-tenth that afforded to orchestras in Berlin, Munich, Vienna, Paris and Amsterdam.

The financial plight of British orchestras becomes apparent when one looks at the experience of orchestras in most other countries. For example, whereas the London Philharmonic Orchestra receives only 12 per cent of its income from state or local government and has to find the remaining 88 per cent from other sources, almost the exact reverse applies to most European orchestras. The big American orchestras are equally well funded, although their substantial backing comes from private and business sponsorship. The LPO in 1979/80 had a budget of £1.5 million, of which 53.4 per cent came from concerts, recordings and other engagements, 17.4 per cent from the box-office, 1.6 per cent from the sale of programmes and advertising, 17.5 per cent from state and local authority grants, leaving 7.2 per cent to be obtained from sponsorship.

The 'market' price of London concerts – roughly, the sum (up to £10,000) an orchestra will lose putting on a well-attended concert without the aid of sponsors – was put under pressure when in 1980 British American Tobacco (BAT) Industries (the UK-based tobacco group) announced that it was giving £600,000 to the Philharmonia Orchestra over two years in a deal to promote its du Maurier brand of cigarettes. Since this sum went to approximately 60 concerts, the price for each suddenly rocketed to £10,000, an artificial figure, of course, since no doubt the Philharmonia found other uses for the money. It was interesting that BAT considered having what was, in effect, its own orchestra to be of such marketing significance. BAT Industries had a total turnover in tobacco of more than £4.2 billion in 1979, but did not compete in the UK market until 1978 because of a long-standing agreement with Imperial Tobacco who, by then, had established a significant lead in the sponsorship field.

The company spent heavily on promoting its State Express brand, especially in sport, but had still achieved no more than 3 per cent of the total market. Clearly, having an orchestra was more than just a gleam in the chairman's eye, and the most immediate, visible effect was the sudden transformation of Philharmonia promotional literature and posters into du Maurier red and silver, and, inevitably, the Philharmonia became referred to by less fortunate rivals as 'the du Maurier band'. The deal gave BAT up-market exposure at a fraction of normal marketing costs precisely when new government curbs on cigarette advertising were being interpreted by many as the harbingers of even more stringent controls, perhaps even an all-out legislative ban.

The scale of BAT's support was shown by the Philharmonia's annual turnover of about £1.5 million. What worried some people in music was that the sponsorship from one source represented 20 per cent of the orchestra's income. Ideally, orchestras should strive for a 'club' of reliable, long-term sponsors of, say, five or six companies per orchestra, each prepared to make at least a three-year commitment.

Mr Christopher Bishop, then the orchestra's energetic Managing Director, was understandably elated, describing the sponsorship as 'a life-line for the Philharmonia'. One hoped that the life-line would not become a noose. For the Philharmonia, the money wiped out a worrying deficit and provided funds for its own marketing operations. But the Philharmonia had other sponsors, such as GKN, Trust House Forte and Datsun. Inevitably, their choice of concerts was dramatically curtailed by the large-scale invasion of BAT, and one wondered whether they would still be around if (as can happen) the du Maurier brand did not reach its targets and BAT decided to try another approach two years later.

Sponsoring a national orchestra, such as the LPO, offers a sponsor a wide choice because such orchestras have an international as well as a national and regional role. Their standards have to be excellent in order to attract outstanding national and international talent, to compete with overseas orchestras and to match world standards. Sir Georg Solti would not have agreed to become the LPO's resident conductor had he not felt it to be Britain's leading orchestra and capable of bearing comparison with those in Chicago, Berlin and Amsterdam.

To preserve its international stature and, in a real sense, to act as unofficial ambassadors for its country, an orchestra needs to undertake overseas tours from time to time. The British Council, which itself spends more than £2.5 million each year in support of arts events overseas, points out that, on average, for every £1 invested from public or private funds in drama, dance and music tours, at least £3 of business is generated and at least £2 returns to Britain in foreign exchange.

Every year Commercial Union, as the LPO's major sponsor, had a choice of Festival Hall concerts and I discussed this with Stephen Crabtree, who succeeded Eric Bravington as Managing Director in 1980. Stephen, a first rate musician, had played double-bass in the orchestra for 12 years before applying his energies and musical knowledge to administration. This was an LPO tradition: Eric Bravington had been an LPO trumpet player for many years. We also reviewed forthcoming tours, looking as far ahead as four or five years. Regional tours were particularly appealing to a company with offices in most towns and cities, and, similarly, it is useful for the orchestra to know when planning overseas tours which parts of the world are most relevant to its sponsors.

For example, since a large slice of CU business derived from the United States, it was natural for us to take the LPO on their 1976 Bicentennial Tour of the USA, and we commissioned Dr Malcolm Arnold, the eminent British composer, to write a special concerto for the occasion, which took the form of a musical tribute to two centuries of American independence. It had its première at the Royal Festival Hall and was played on many radio stations in the United States during and after the tour.

We started planning the US tour some two years earlier, and an incident that occurred some months before departure demonstrated the way a business sponsorship partnership can provide unexpected benefits for the group being sponsored. One Sunday evening the telephone rang in my home in Bedfordshire. Eric Bravington was on the line and he sounded concerned.

'Vic, bad news. I'm afraid we shall have to cancel the American visit,' he said bleakly. He then explained that a dramatic increase in air fares and other expenses had made nonsense of the estimated budget. 'To make the trip now,' he said, 'we'd need twice the amount of sponsorship money you've agreed to put up and obviously we can't expect that. We've just had a Board meeting and I wanted you to know the situation right away. We'll cancel the tour at once and this will at least give us a little time to fill the dates with UK engagements.'

After a moment's thought I asked Eric to postpone a decision for 24 hours. Next morning I discussed the problem with CU's Chairman, Sir Francis Sandilands. He immediately agreed that we should not let the LPO down. By 10 a.m. I had telephoned Eric Bravington to tell him to confirm the tour and that CU would double its sponsorship.

This incident, more than anything, convinced the LPO that sponsorship was more than simply writing out a cheque and that we would prove staunch friends in a crisis (foreshadowing the slogan later used by CU's UK marketing division). Of course, it is possible to avoid such situations. When we decided to sponsor the Orchestra's fiftieth anniversary tour of European capitals in 1983, we began financing the operation some years ahead. Annual payments were put on deposit by the LPO in a separate tour fund to earn interest and so meet anticipated inflation increases.

This sort of involvement in an orchestra's long-term artistic and financial policies allows a sponsor to match his own objectives with those of the orchestra, and it promotes a healthy and continuing relationship. Like most sponsors in Britain, we took pains to remain separate from the artistic side of a sponsored organisation for the excellent reason that we are not qualified to offer advice. It was not our business and would have created all sorts of sinister vibrations. But not everyone shares this view.

After the Association for Business Sponsorship of the Arts (ABSA) was established in 1976 by two or three leading companies, including Commercial Union, I was visited by someone wishing to launch a similar sponsorship information bureau overseas. An hour's discussion concluded with this final, and quite serious, question: 'How much do you, as a sponsor, take part in selecting the programme to be played by an orchestra or the plays to be performed by a theatrical company?' The visitor seemed genuinely astonished when I explained that we played no part in this at all. 'But you're paying the piper. Surely you have a preference for Beethoven, perhaps, or Berlioz, and want to make sure that they are featured in your concerts?'

Apart from the ethics of preserving artistic integrity, there are sound reasons for not trying to influence artistic directors even if they were prepared to listen. A sponsor promoting a dud play or a disastrous concert is in enough trouble without also being held responsible for the artistic content. He is likely to get some flak anyway and must be prepared to deal with loaded questions, as he does in any other area of public affairs.

After the first night of Scottish Opera's inventive and, as some said, daring production of *Rigoletto* which we sponsored, a BBC radio interviewer asked: 'How do you feel about sponsoring the first opera to be booed at Glasgow's Theatre Royal?' We both knew that, in fact, the overwhelming audience reception had been enthusiastic. Two people (one from a rival opera company) had made token noises of disapproval which few others even heard.

To have been drawn into that argument would have been fatal. The reaction instead was to smile and reply 'We knew that some people might not approve of seeing their old favourite presented in an untraditional way and we sympathise with their views. But most people thoroughly enjoyed the performance and if it provokes a lively response, whether for or against, we feel it has succeeded. That's what the theatre and opera are about, after all.' The interviewer grinned. Honours were even and we went on to discuss other matters.

Afterwards, I reflected that perhaps sponsors *are* making artistic decisions of a kind, for non-artistic reasons. Obviously, when sponsoring an opera and hoping to appeal to a wide audience, including staff, one is likely to decline *Wozzeck* and bid for *La Traviata* (which, indeed, we did). Similarly, we would rather have supported a cultural event in Boston (where CU had its United States head office) than in Philadelphia. CU did support the Boston Symphony and Ballet.

Sadly, Commercial Union is no longer a significant sponsor. Having established itself as a leading sponsor of the arts and sport, it has since 1983 largely dropped out of both. This withdrawal was due to a combination of poor trading experience, especially in the United States, and a change of senior management. General cost-cutting, which is not always the same thing as saving, was introduced, and this incident shows how important it is for a sponsored organisation to avoid relying on one major sponsor. Fortunately, CU's withdrawal from various sponsorship commitments was done gradually in order to minimise the impact. The Prudential subsequently became the LPO's chief supporter.

Opera and ballet can be an extremely effective way of reaching an up-market target audience. Some of the most rewarding sponsorships are found in these arts, though the cost is high and some claim that the sponsor's needs and expectations are not always given adequate consideration. I have heard people complain about a take-it-or-leave-it attitude shown by some opera companies, which seemed to be saying 'Well, we *are* rather special, so you should feel privileged being allowed to sponsor us'. I do not think that such an attitude is widespread or that it would ever be encountered above junior administrator level and it would be a pity if potential sponsors allowed themselves to be deterred by such irritations.

At the operatic pinnacle Britain has such prized possessions as the Royal Opera House, Covent Garden, and the unique Glyndebourne, both entirely different, funded differently, yet each preserving the highest standards and with an enviable record of charming money from the vaults of industry. Why are they so special? What is the justification for what may seem like a disproportionately large slice of the sponsorship cake falling on their plates?

Sir Claus Moser, statistician, banker, enthusiastic amateur musician and then Chairman of the Royal Opera House, put the case a few years back:

If a country wants a major international house performing opera and ballet, it is expensive. Actually, the Royal Opera House, which in a year spends between £11 million and £12 million, is considerably cheaper than comparable houses abroad like the New York Met., Paris or Vienna, or even Munich or La Scala.

Point two is that if one wants to be in the international league – and we like to think we're near the top for both opera and ballet – one must not risk falling standards. So, unavoidably, such an operation costs a great deal more than, say, the theatre, which has small casts, much cheaper scenery, no orchestra, no chorus, far fewer stage hands, etc. The question is really 'Does Britain want an international opera/ballet house?' If so, it's got to be paid for.

The cheapest ticket at Covent Garden costs £7 and the reason that the price is not higher is that there is a public subsidy (worth roughly half the real cost). The most expensive seats cost £70. The subsidy figure for opera houses on the Continent would be up to 80 per cent. Artists' fees help to make opera expensive and top singers can earn more than £1,000 a night. Yet fees are not the largest proportion of the total expenditure and amount to something around 15 per cent. Most expenditure goes on running costs and the wages and salaries of 1,000 staff and these are not high by international standards.

Covent Garden points out that the bulk (55 per cent) of the financial aid is from the State, and only about 3 per cent comes from the private sector. Yet, any business wishing to sponsor a Covent Garden production must think in terms of around £50,000 before adding on the cost of tickets for guests, receptions and 'beefing up' the poster advertising that the Royal Opera House cannot afford or is unwilling to do on a large scale (since they have no problem in selling their tickets).

This sum is dwarfed by the amount of money raised on behalf of the Royal Opera House building development scheme: something around £9 million, about half from the private sector. Mr Norman St John-Stevas, when Arts Minister, added his voice to the appeal calling upon 'those firms and individuals who have not yet contributed to the full extent that they are able to come forward now.' This was a remarkable evangelical statement by a Minister on behalf of one organisation, and Covent Garden's own village fête – a royal gala auction attended by Prince Charles and Princess Margaret – saw the sale of works of art, furniture, silver, porcelain, rare wines and a £55,000 Rolls Royce, with profits going to the ROH fund.

Understandable envy must be aroused in the encampments of the theatre, that more traditional British art form. It does attract sponsorship but, so far, not with the consistent success of music and sport. One can see the difficulties all too clearly.

When a commercial company puts its money into any form of art, it wants that event to be successful. Bad reviews are unimportant compared with empty houses, and, whereas in music it is possible to make accurate assessments of likely success or failure, nobody has yet devised a foolproof method of determining whether a play is going to cause rapture or rupture at the box-office. The stage, more than almost anything else in the arts, can arouse public controversy, and controversy is usually bad for business. It therefore has a tough task dispelling the sponsor's nightmare of seeing his company linked to some semi-pornographic assault on private enterprise and the British way-of-life when he thought he was getting into nothing more daring than *Private Lives* or *Night Must Fall*.

Trident Television sponsored a new play at the Old Vic, *The 88*, but, when reviews suggested this was a dicey subject, Trident's name swiftly came off the publicity. Undaunted, Trident came back to support *Macbeth* with Peter O'Toole (an offer that I had declined) only to be greeted by a resounding raspberry from the critics. And Trident Television, presumably, had access to more informed opinion on the theatre and current tastes. I had some sympathy for the consultant trying to sell me an excellent sponsorship package on behalf of the National Theatre, at a time when the press and the Chairman of the Greater London Council were, for once, united in outraged condemnation of a current production at the Olivier, featuring blood, gore, homosexual rape, pubic display, misrepresented history and, worse still, windy rhetoric.

Yet, the theatre communicates more directly with people than other art forms: it is more easily understood and relates much more to everyday life. Potentially, it has probably more to offer, therefore, and it is in desperate need of funding. Take the late lamented Old Vic Company as an example. It had no subsidy from the Arts Council for its work in London (and its £300,000 touring subsidy was axed in the 1981 cut-back) but received grants totalling £100,000 from the boroughs of Southwark and Lambeth and from the GLC. In comparison, grants to the National Theatre were then nearly £3.5 million and to the Royal Shakespeare Company nearly £2 million.

The Old Vic's time-honoured policy was to offer cheap seats to young people, which meant lost income on the face value of a ticket. It subsidised this activity through sponsorship, or by increasing the price of seats sold to other members of the public. Associate Director, Jack Emery, told me that in an average winter season the Old Vic gave 40 matinées and lost £1,900 per performance on the face value of tickets it made available to the local education authorities at the cheap rate of £2 apiece. Thus, in a season the total loss could be £76,000, assuming, of course, that all the seats were sold. Many schools prefer to bring their pupils to evening performances, and the 10 per cent reduction given to school parties meant a loss on box-office returns that reached £30,000 over the same winter period. Said Emery, 'We must face the unpalatable prospect of having to discontinue children's matinées and other concessions for schools without some major subsidy – in other words, young people may be excluded from this theatre on the grounds of cost.' Alas, in April 1981 the Old Vic ceased operations.

Here, surely, was an opportunity for enlightened sponsorship to ensure that there would always be some cheap seats that schools and individual students could afford. It seems a natural for a nationwide service industry with a need to demonstrate its social responsibility and which also has a keen eye on tomorrow's consumer. The Old Vic had run a successful subscription ticket system, and the expensive pilot survey was sponsored by Imperial Tobacco. Ticket prices are a vexed question and it has been estimated that, if pre-war prices in Britain had kept pace with inflation, a West End theatre ticket would cost between £20 and £25, or more than twice what it is now.

Not all theatre opportunities have to be in London. Excellent provincial companies can offer high standards, big audiences and a recognisable publicity return for sponsorship money. The Cambridge Arts Theatre Company, for instance, gets good reviews from the dourest critics, and employs stars like Maxine Audley, James Bolam, Eleanor Bron, Tom Conti, Michael Gough, Wendy Hiller, Ian McKellan and Virginia McKenna to play leading roles, persuading them to work sometimes for £100 per week compared to the £500 to £1,000 they would receive in the West End. Why does it need subsidies and sponsorship?

There are several reasons. As we have seen, seat prices are artificially low, but the Arts Council grant that makes this possible is given to the Cambridge company to play in 'middle-scale' touring theatres, which would otherwise see few high-quality productions. 'Middle-scale' means 400 to 900 seats; in other words, too small to be profitable, hence the Arts Council grant. If every seat were sold for every performance throughout the year at the Arts Theatre, Cambridge, the theatre would *still* lose money. To put on a Shakespeare play costs about £65,000 and only £29,000 can be recouped at the box-office. The Theatre is unlikely to get more government subsidy in the present economic climate, and business sponsorship is the only hope.

The Theatre provided me with a typical budget for a Shakespeare or major classic (see Table 6.1). It is extremely instructive.

Table 6.1 Example of Cambridge Arts Theatre early 1980s budget to allow for 18 actors rehearsing for four weeks, playing in Cambridge for two weeks and touring for four weeks; plus a stage-management team of six

Item	£
Salaries plus NI for 18 actors, 6 stage management for 10 weeks, plus holiday pay for a 10-week engagement (as per Equity agreement)	26,673
Fees for director, designer, lighting designer, carpenter	1,810
Rail fares	3,596
Living allowance (Equity minimum)	8,220
Scenery	5,000
Props and furniture	1,610
Costumes and wigs	4,360
Sound recording and equipment hire	600
Rehearsal room hire	480
Publicity and advertising	3,600
Stage management running expenses, scripts and public relations entertainment	1,070
Transport and handling of scenery	3,750
Author's royalties (10% of gross takings)	2,900
Contigency	1,673
Total expenditure	£65,342
Total estimated income	£29,000

Museum curators sometimes complain wistfully that business sponsorship rarely comes their way. The situation is different in the United States, where tax laws encourage businessmen to endow such places handsomely, and occasionally, in return, they get their name attached to an edifice which then becomes their own memorial – a relatively harmless piece of vanity.

British museums have come a long way and done much to get rid of their dull, fusty image. Many of them now employ an education or schools liaison officer and encourage visits from parties of young people. However, they seem to have made little effort to woo business sponsors. Of the hundreds of approaches I received each year, only one or two came from museums. This is surprising when one thinks of childhood wonder at the Science and Natural History Museums in Kensington or the old London Museum, full of animated history that stimulated imagination. Americans and Canadians do far better, often with less promising material, and British museums could learn much from them.

The shining examples of museum sponsorship are the great touring exhibitions. These were expertly managed and not only paid for themselves but yielded the sponsor a cash profit, not to mention television and press coverage and excellent public relations. Tutankhamun, Ancient China, the gold of El Dorado have all been presented with varying degrees of success, but few have excelled the Pompeii Exhibition, seen at London's Royal Academy by 630,000 people and sponsored by Imperial Tobacco and the *Daily Telegraph*. In Chapter 9 there is a full description of how this exhibition was planned and serviced to obtain maximum benefit.

Apart from annual prizes and awards, literature is largely an undiscovered land for sponsors. One does not include here support given by such firms as W. H. Smith, which is, after all, a form of promotion for its own products. Increased leisure might revive reading habits, if television's conquest of our minds is really only temporary, and so lure sponsors into the field.

However, if I were asked to say which field I thought offered the greatest potential to the arts sponsor, I would answer popular music with its vast audience of youngsters. Things have already started to happen.

When Manhattan Transfer put on a special charity show at London's Dominion in 1979 the concert was funded by Akai, the Japanese electronics and hi-fi giant. Davidson, the American motor cycle manufacturers, subsidised the rock group Judas Priest, and the 35-date British tour by Genesis in 1980 was underwritten by a brewery so that the cheaper tickets could be pegged to £2.

The pop industry, for so long the affluent prodigal of the entertainment industry, able to turn its nose up at sponsorship, is now beginning to suffer from rising costs and look for industrial support. For every successful album, hundreds are released and never recoup their costs. World tours can cripple even top-of-the-chart bank balances. Thin Lizzy's 1979 UK tour was a sell-out weeks in advance, grossed £250,000 in ticket sales and still lost £21,000.

I interviewed the Marquess of Tavistock at his ancestral home, Woburn Abbey, the morning after 200,000 people had turned up for an open-air concert by Neil Diamond. Something like £25,000 went into Woburn's coffers and £250,000 went to Mr Diamond.

'But of course it cost him that to put the show on, pay for all his staff, hotels, coaches, lighting and so on,' said the Marquess. Ironically, I recalled talking to the Marquess's father, the Duke of Bedford, 20 years earlier, when he had just inherited Woburn Abbey and was planning how to meet the daunting death duties and pay the enormous costs of maintaining the Abbey and its lovely grounds.

Mr Diamond's budget made even Woburn's running costs seem moderate. But Mr Diamond no doubt derived his income from selling a million records (at £1 profit each?). Life is indeed rum when a motor cycle manufacturer will put up £½ million to fund a pop group on tour, while one of the world's leading symphony orchestras is losing £4,000 every time it plays to a capacity audience at the Royal Festival Hall.

Finally, one should not overlook the possibilities of sponsoring the visual arts. Private sponsors sometimes invest money by financing a young artist in whom they have faith (and hope for a return on their investment in the future), but companies can do art and themselves some good by financing art exhibitions. Even more satisfying was a scheme that I started some years ago, under which a company bought prints by young artists and put them on display in its offices and subsequently gave them to schools and hospitals. This offered the artist a helping hand and provided him with a wider audience.

CHAPTER 7

Sponsorship objectives

While a sense of social obligation must be part of any sponsorship philosophy and, indeed, fundamental to support for the arts, it is idle to pretend that this is the sole motivation. Dr Johnson's remark is apposite: 'To act from pure benevolence is not possible for finite beings. Human benevolence is mingled with vanity, interest or some other motive.'

In a competitive market a company's priority must be success in its particular field. And is this not also a basic social responsibility? Success safeguards the jobs of employees, the savings of investors and improves the service available to customers. Business sponsorship should, therefore, be seen as a help towards achieving this success, although it is not true that 'The only excuse for sponsorship is sales, and the only excuse for sales is profit', to paraphrase the marketing maxim.

Sponsorship and marketing are linked to other aspects of corporate life, for today the role of commerce is becoming more complicated. A company's actions are judged by many audiences in addition to employees, shareholders and customers, and sponsorship affects, or is affected by, all forms of public relations activities as well as marketing goals.

While marketing men often have to achieve results within a short time-scale to justify expenditure, public relations executives operate at a more strategic level and, since every contact between industry and the world outside offers an opportunity for both good and bad public relations, they are taking a hard look at sponsorship which is establishing itself as an area in which a company can develop its relations with the public and do much else besides. The companies which will find sponsorship most interesting are the well-founded companies which are sure enough in their current market positions to be able to draw up ten-year plans. It would be a sensible move to undertake a sponsorship campaign directed at the younger generation. After all, today's youth is tomorrow's market.

At some stage sponsorship may involve community relations, trade relations, government relations, internal staff relations, advertising and press relations and education contacts.

Any newcomer to sponsorship should be absolutely clear about his aims and expectations, and know why he has selected sponsorship as a part of his marketing mix. This seems axiomatic, yet many companies going into sponsorship for the first time really have not thought out the process to anything like this extent.

Some time ago Alastair Sedgwick, one of the gurus of sporting and other sponsorship activities and the man who helped to create the Gillette Cup, invited me to one of his mini-seminars in Chelsea to listen to some leading spenders expounding their views on arts sponsorship. Sedgwick, whose wife, Nina, is a concert pianist, listened politely as one advertising manager argued vehemently against diverting any of his company's money away from the advertising budget to sponsorship.

Alastair then made a few points. With his permission I quote them at length:

Let it be said right away, that for those who consider their advertising budget is insufficient to achieve their tactical goals, sponsorship is hardly for them. Sponsorship, at least arts sponsorship, is not a substitute for market place advertising. It is, however, if properly applied, a very valuable tiller of the soil in which to plant one's advertising seeds, or in dealing, if you permit a further horticultural metaphor, with established plants, it can be a means of ensuring they benefit from adequate exposure to the sun.

It is the ill-considered adoption of sponsorship of the arts that creates most misgivings at a later stage. So often more is expected than can be delivered or than has been invested in time, money and effort by the company concerned.

It is not enough, in responding to the compelling clarion call of the Minister for the Arts, for Industry to assume that by entering the arts arena, they immediately qualify for the prize of Victor Ludorum. Sponsorship needs marketing if a company wants a noticeable return from its investment. If it does not, then it's not sponsorship, but patronage, and none the worse for that, as far as the arts are concerned.

But as always with marketing, you must determine to whom you are marketing, before you can rightly apply the 'sponsorship' remedy.

Has the company a community relations problem? In which case it is likely the sponsorship must have a strong local application. Or is it, perhaps, a problem of government relations, of finding common ground or atmosphere, in which to put over a viewpoint to a key official who might be more conducive and relaxed when lulled by a Mozart serenade? He might even consider the sales director as almost human if he shares an appreciation of the finer points of a Scarlatti sonata when played on the pianoforte and not, as is traditional, on the harpsichord.

At the same seminar spokesmen for three major companies, a bank, a manufacturer and a leading computer giant, gave these reasons for investing in the arts.

The man from Lloyds felt that an organisation that relied more than most on its good reputation needed to be seen to be making a sensible contribution to society. 'That is why', he added, 'we concentrate on helping the young – mainly through education, the arts and conservation – and stay away from sport, professional cultural organisations and the wilder flights of fancy of those who think they should have our money.'

A spokesman for Martini & Rossi pointed to his company's 15-year involvement and added that, while the Arts Council's support is essential to keep art alive, it is also industry's responsibility to aid those arts wherever possible and so enable this country to maintain its great traditions of entertainment.

The IBM man opined that a greater involvement by business in the mainstream of society was not only inevitable, but desirable. Arts sponsorship enabled IBM to make a contribution to the quality of life and, through support to events outside London, to involve itself more closely in the life of the communities where it had locations and offices.

It was interesting and not insignificant that even those three large and experienced business sponsors still apparently differed in their views on who should be responsible within their own organisations for such a vital function. The three speakers included a head of public relations, a director of advertising and a personnel manager.

Now, supposing a business sponsor decides that, purely for marketing reasons, he would like to get his company into this expanding field before all the best buys have been snapped up by competitors. On the face of it sponsorship has everything a marketing director is looking for. It has the excitement and glamour to attract high visibility and possible television coverage; it has prestige and it is fun. It can attract an enormous amount of publicity and it is relatively inexpensive. Why, then, has it proved, for some companies, a big disappointment?

First and most obviously, when a sponsorship scheme fails it was probably a bad idea from the beginning and doomed to disaster. This could mean that the scheme and the sponsor were ill-matched, which suggests that insufficient thought and research preceded the decision to sponsor. Such failures are becoming fewer as greater experience is gained and more and more companies realise the importance of developing their own corporate philosophy on sponsorship. This makes it so much simpler to identify the schemes that will be most appropriate to their needs and therefore cost-beneficial. The next most common factor in failure is the mishandling of a good idea, either by the sponsor or the sponsored body, and all sorts of things from lack of policy control and sheer ignorance to personality clashes can play a part.

Sports sponsorship offers the most exposure to both success and failure, and among the more publicised disappointments was the Colt Car company's brief flirtation with the Grand National: they withdrew after sponsoring it for a year, disappointed at the amount of publicity it yielded.

John Carson, Marketing Director of Schweppes, was correct when he said that many companies go into sports sponsorship for the wrong reasons and pay the inevitable penalty. He was very critical of British companies for their lack of professionalism in this area and compared them unfavourably with companies in the United States and Australia, where sponsorship is a much much more widely accepted activity. Carson's opinion was based on long experience and a fairly hard-nosed, commercial approach.

Schweppes regarded its sponsorship programme as a vitally important part of its overall marketing strategy, while realising that the rewards were not always as tangible as those from an advertising campaign. In 1979 it spent 3.5 per cent of its marketing budget on sponsorship, and its objectives included extra sales, publicity, an enhanced image, increased awareness, a closeness to the community and an opportunity to entertain customers in attractive surroundings. Schweppes' largest involvement in a single sporting activity was its sponsorship of the County Cricket Championship, then officially renamed the Schweppes County Championship, although not all newspapers were prepared to admit this fact at first. Such irritations are less common in sport than in the arts. When in 1980 we launched the Commercial Union Junior World Cup for under-18 golfers, the only newspapers to omit the company name from their reports were the *Daily Mail* and the *Straits Times* in Singapore. Carson admitted the difficulty of evaluating rewards, and he told *Marketing Week*

If you believe that sponsoring something is instantly going to win friends, influence people and generate sales towards your produce . . . you just can't be absolutely sure. A sponsor can commission detailed market research to find out what the public thinks about his activities, but that can sometimes cost as much as the actual sponsorship. In our view, no market research company has ever done it effectively – and I speak for other major sponsors as well. There is an opportunity for new business here.

It should be added that Schweppes' visibility is so high in its own particular market that any increase resulting from sponsorship would be marginal, so image-building applies less in its case.

However, since that interview Carson has become more specific. Of the objectives identified above, the one most satisfactorily attained by cricket sponsorship was publicity. He calculated that Schweppes received column inches in the sports pages worth £2 million.

This is a tempting argument for advocates of sponsorship and one that is, not surprisingly, extremely irksome to advertising executives. When Commercial Union ran the international lawn tennis Grand Prix I remember doing a similar calculation at the Masters Final in Stockholm in 1975, when Ilie Nastase caused some embarrassment by demolishing the then nervous young warrior Bjorn Borg in front of the King of Sweden. The Masters was booked for several hours' television coverage worldwide (the Grand Prix ran to much more) but, concentrating only on the film of the event put out by the BBC at peak viewing time, we calculated that Commerical Union received exposure that, at advertising rates, would have cost literally millions of pounds!

Such comparisons are somewhat false because advertisers cannot buy unlimited viewing time, and the BBC does not take advertising anyway. Even so, when advertising agencies object to what they regard as the naive practice of directly comparing paid-for advertising space with free editorial coverage, they forget that almost every sponsor will regard publicity as an important and probably a primary purpose of this form of marketing activity.

It is, indeed, claimed that the main purpose of sports sponsorship is to get television coverage. This is open to argument, and marketing men will point out that the product name is normally seen only in a static, two-dimensional context even when you *do* have TV coverage. And there is no guarantee that you will get the coverage you want or expect. As I write this, a BBC television news reader has just mentioned in almost the same breath 'the John Player Cricket Cup' and a raft race on the Tay 'sponsored by a Scotch whisky firm', thus neatly summing up the Corporation's ambivalent attitude to sponsorship.

Sponsorship is not a substitute for television (or any other) advertising. Compare the £200 million investment it represents with the £4,000 million spent on advertising in the United Kingdom. It may *arise* naturally out of a TV campaign and meet some marketing objectives. It can be used to *complement* orthodox advertising but not necessarily to replace it. Martini's sponsorship of skiing or fencing, for example, accorded well with the personality created by its advertising. Du Maurier's link with the Philharmonia was to 'enhance the elegance and style' of its cigarette. Schweppes may have benefited more from effervescent, one-day cricket than from more reflective, three-day county championships. Dunhill reinforced its image as a market leader by identification with Masters events. The flip approach was exemplified by Bryant & May's sponsorship of the play *The Matchmaker*.

Does sponsorship actually sell any products? Few can say, although two companies who believe that sponsorship has had a significant impact on public awareness of their existence are Zanussi, the Italian manufacturers of domestic appliances, and Cornhill Insurance.

In 1979 Zanussi sponsored an unsuccessful British attempt to cross the Atlantic by hot-air balloon, even though they had been strongly advised against getting involved with such a hazardous project. Apart from manufacturers of hot-air balloons, balloon fabrics, fuel or baskets, few people immediately suggest themselves as ideal customers for this form of sponsorship.

Matching horses for courses is something that does not deter those seeking sponsorship. Insurance companies are sometimes approached by organisers of such high-risk activities as motor car racing, parachuting and so on, ignoring the philosophy of insurance which is to reduce the risk of calamity as well as lessen its effects. It is sometimes necessary to explain to eager marketing men why it would be imprudent to have an insurance company logo on boxes of matches which, in infant hands, could cause fire and tragedy. Similarly, banks should, logically, steer clear of sports with a high gambling association.

In fact, Zanussi considered its decision was justified, even though the Translantic attempt failed. It believed it achieved much in overcoming a particular problem, which at that time was lack of public awareness of its existence or what it did. Zanussi's Managing Director, George Dorman, commented that the balloon flight made the headlines for five days and subsequent research suggested that 62 per cent of the public knew about the company compared with 36 per cent before the balloon went up.

Insurance companies frequently make a success of cricket sponsorship. Prudential, fortunate when the sun shone on its original one-day enterprise, has deserved its publicity acclaim, and another well-timed sponsorship coup was Cornhill's dramatic intervention to snatch English cricket from the jaws of the old barracuda himself, Kerry Packer, by sponsoring Test cricket in England.

Some people may ask 'Why a comparative insurance minnow like Cornhill rather than big fish such as Commercial Union and the Royal?' As far as CU is concerned, the answer was simply that an international group operating around the world in about 100 different countries must prefer a sport with the widest possible international appeal. Lawn tennis and golf could, therefore, have preference when it comes to decisions of that kind, in the same way that music is regarded as an international language, and is therefore more appropriate than poetry reading or legitimate theatre.

Cornhill claimed to have increased its 'public awareness' figure from 2 per cent to 16 per cent, which is not bad in a traditionally reticent industry that generally excites little public interest except when premium rates go up.

Like other beginners to sponsorship, Cornhill found that the initial fee was only part of the overall cost. It agreed to spend £1 million over five years but did not take into account below-the-line costs, such as advertising, public relations, printing and entertaining. Even so, Cornhill's is undoubtedly one of the more successful efforts, and at least one envious marketing executive was said to have remarked 'I reckon they've put in £3 million and it's won them £25 million worth of business.' Other wilder guesses have been made. However, once related advertising and management costs were included, that original £1 million could easily have reached the predicted £3 million by 1982 when the five years elapsed, and when, if some estimates were accurate, more than £75 million in new business would have been earned.

The results in financial terms will always defy quantification one suspects, but in less tangible ways they must be significant. I wonder what other form of campaign would have given an 800 per cent increase in public awareness in under two years, and at what cost?

This is not forgetting the other side of the coin. One retains the memory of Cornhill staff pickets parading outside the Oval during a Test match. Their banners pointed out that, while the company was spending £400,000 a year on cricket, it was, so they alleged, being less than generous in current wage negotiations with its own employees. The fact that sponsorship funds, even if diverted into wage packets, would have little effect on them, or that, as part of a marketing campaign, the money is better spent in promoting business and thus underpinning salaries in the long term, is an esoteric argument that cannot compete with emotive banners, especially at a time of rising unemployment.

If sponsorship is to take its part in a highly competitive, cost- and profit-conscious marketing campaign, it has to be thoroughly professional in planning and execution. Handled with flair, it can give a fresh appeal and a cutting edge to a marketing mix. The age when companies sponsored racing because the chairman owned a racehorse, or supported motor rallies because the corporate affairs director was a sports car fanatic is behind us. But it is equally short-sighted to follow the herd and go into cricket or table tennis because somebody else appears to be doing well at it. Each company must analyse for itself the reasons, likely benefits and problems, and do so in its own market context.

When talking of the 'marketing mix' one includes branding, sales presentation, promotions, exhibitions, advertising, identification and so on. Advertisers and agencies know the importance of identifying customer needs, of researching how successfully a product meets those needs, correct presentation, building awareness, trial, re-purchase, trade loyalty and so on. But the process also demands imagination to transform adequate marketing into successful marketing.

Barclays Bank, for example, is highly decentralised; it has given its 35 or so local head offices discretionary limits, which they can then spend in their local communities. They therefore go for local sponsorship projects, leaving national projects to the bank's London head office. The Bank uses commercial sponsorship to aid business development, as for example its sponsorship of the Royal Smithfield Show. Agriculture is a lucrative business sector and exposure in the farming community, which the show must offer, is good for business. Similarly, Barclaycard sponsored Recro '80, Britain's first international leisure festival at the royal showground, Stoneleigh, committing £100,000 to the project.

The Bank thinks a set sponsorship budget is too restrictive and prefers making *ad hoc* decisions. This may make it easier to respond to unsolicited requests but is not an ideal way to run a sponsorship pro-gramme. It favours events outside London, helping the Glyndebourne touring company, and giving £120,000 over a three-year period to the D'Oyly Carte touring company.

When Volvo, the Swedish car firm, took over the lawn tennis Grand Prix it was a decision based on hard-headed advice from a group of American marketing experts called the Boston Consulting Group. They devised a simple diagrammatic method to find the right sponsorship for Volvo and it led them into lawn tennis, show jumping, golf and yachting.

Volvo cars had a dependable but somewhat staid public image. When a novelist writes of the City business commuters streaming off the 6.25 train at Surbiton and heading for 'the waiting Volvos' he is striking a nerve that all marketing men must have. To find out how to change that image and reach a wider market, a diagram with crucial alternatives was drawn (see Figure 7.1).

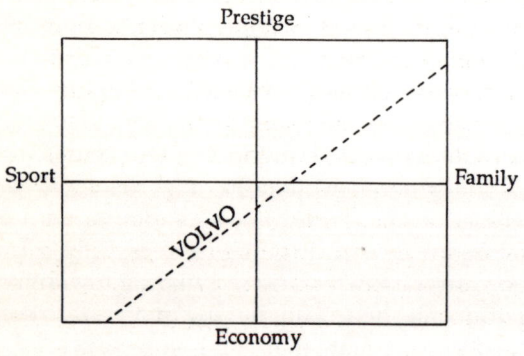

Fig. 7.1   The diagram that persuaded Volvo to turn its sales drive towards tennis

While Sport *versus* Family, and Prestige *versus* Economy in Figure 7.1 are not precise opposites, their compatibility is open to doubt. For example, when you buy a Rolls you don't automatically check the fuel consumption. Similarly, sports car fanatics are not too bothered about the lack of leg room for Aunt Mabel or if the back seat accommodation is strictly limited. When the diagonal line representing the company profile was drawn, Volvo cars fell decidedly between Family and Economy, which could scarcely have come as a surprise. Prestige and Sport were perhaps considered irrational values, but they happened to be important in the market that Volvo wished to capture. A market survey reported, 'The profile of a Volvo customer shows him or her to be highly educated with high income. This is true of people around tennis.'

Volvo's entry into sport had been heralded with a £200,000-a-year show jumping sponsorship held in ten countries. The company's subsequent golf sponsorship in Sweden was almost too successful because Volvo began to turn golf into a potential mass-interest sport and the company was not interested in the mass market.

As one Volvo executive said, 'It doesn't really matter whether or not the ordinary man in the street knows Volvo. He's not our customer. That's why we stopped mass TV advertising in the United States. It was getting us nowhere.' Volvo has since moved into the small family-car market and switched back into top-level golf sponsorship in order to reach the required mass audiences.

The move into lawn tennis in 1980 was made with characteristic style and flourish. Even so, it must have been done with some misgivings because the greatest lawn tennis player of the day, Sweden's own Bjorn Borg, could not be part of the team. He was already signed up by Volvo's Swedish rival, Saab, to endorse their car. Volvo spent well over £1 million on their first year of lawn tennis sponsorship.

Another firm with clear-cut objectives in sponsorship is Benson & Hedges, which ranks probably as the most lavish spender with well over £4 million invested in cricket, lawn tennis, show jumping, angling, golf and music festivals. It will be noted that these are all 'clean' activities and their Special Events Manager confesses that the controversial nature of their product prompts this policy. 'We didn't want to get involved in dirty or noisy sports,' he said. 'We didn't want old ladies getting beaten up after our events. So we stayed away from the tough sports.'

Benson & Hedges is one of the few sponsors who make determined efforts to measure the effect of their sponsorships, monitoring not only their own 'mileage' in the press and on radio and television, but also that of their rivals.

How sponsorship can assist a company's local prestige was demonstrated when Commercial Union took Cantilena, the Scottish chamber music ensemble, under their leader Adrian Shepherd, to South America in 1980. Their playing of Scarlatti, Vivaldi and Boyce was acclaimed by press and public, and special embassy concerts were given for civic leaders in places like Buenos Aires. Similarly, when we arranged an open draw for our 1981 Junior World Cup in Dublin, the function held in the new offices of the Hibernian Insurance Company (in which Commercial Union had a minor holding) was attended by press, radio and TV plus diplomatic representatives from the 16 participating countries, including four ambassadors.

Despite the tremendous increase in sponsorship of all kinds, it is still not possible to evaluate sponsorship precisely. The high cost of research in relation to total sponsorship expenditure – significantly higher than with media advertising – is one factor. Another could be that many marketing experts still believe that sponsorship *cannot* be monitored. They may not yet have accepted the fact that in a changing world marketing must adapt itself to meet the needs of a more sophisticated consumer, who may have grown difficult to persuade by traditional advertising techniques. The reasons for going into sponsorship invariably contain the key to its evaluation. As Dr Elizabeth Nelson, Chairman of Taylor Nelson Group, put it to me: 'If you can tell us exactly why you are spending this money and what you expect to achieve, then we can measure your relative success'. Dr Nelson would probably agree that the sponsor might aim not only to boost sales but also to increase public awareness of his company and improve its image both within the trade and with customers. She also agrees that the chief difference between sponsorship and other forms of promotion is that sponsoring is invariably a long-term activity – often lasting five years. Thus, a £1 million five-year sponsorship would involve an annual outlay of £200,000. A £20,000 evaluation programme would, therefore, seem expensive at 10 per cent of the annual cost. Dr Nelson argues that since the research expenditure is to secure the effectiveness of the total programme it should be amortised over the five years – 2 per cent of the total budget makes much more sense. As we have seen, planning is essential at the earliest stage and that means allowing for a baseline study *before* the sponsorship commences.

Sponsorship statistics are mushrooming, especially of sports sponsorship. Derek Etherington cornered this particular segment of the information market with his twice-yearly publication *Sportscan*, which he owned until selling out to a larger information agency in 1988.

Etherington, a former marketing director of EMI Leisure and Ladbroke Racing, had the simple but brilliant notion that sport on television could be monitored to yield a wealth of facts and figures of immense interest to sponsoring companies, consultants, marketing and advertising agencies, and the media.

Sportscan contains the data on how much television coverage is given to which sports, who sponsors what, who leads in terms of money spent, time on the box, etc. In the early days it was a matter of Derek (or Mrs Etherington) sitting in front of the television with pencil and notepad.

Computers subsequently streamlined the recording and storing of information, although Etherington still devoted weekends to poring over hundreds of newspaper clippings to make sure he was aware of all the latest developments. What may have started as a cottage industry became a shrewd investment for Derek who probably merited some kind of Thatcher award for commercial initiative.

As we shall see in Chapter 8, it is commonsense to make sure that the event sponsored is compatible with your product and that it attracts an audience that, by and large, matches your own customers or the customers you wish to enlist. There have been sad errors. Colgate's massive investment in sponsorship was not matched by a significant increase in the demand for toothpaste, and the Silentnight Company pulled out of sponsoring a golf event after one year. Somehow the public did not realise that it was a mattress company and the sponsorship, understandably, yielded little of value.

CHAPTER 8

Choosing a sponsorship

Cost and value in sponsorship are not necessarily related. Sponsorship success depends almost always upon the perseverance, imagination and sweat of those involved on both sides. But, as the Americans found in the Persian desert, all the effort in the world can be undone by incomplete planning, and choosing the right sponsorship requires at least the same degree of care and forethought that is applied to other management activities within any corporation.

The reason that this does not always happen is partly that sponsorship is still comparatively new, and the skills that now exist have been developed by trial and error in what is largely unexplored territory. In a work-oriented society it is inevitable that sponsored activities such as sport and the arts are treated less than seriously, because we associate them with leisure, relaxation, frivolity. Some mental adjustment is required to alter this subconscious judgement and recognise them as potentially useful aids in the harsher world of commerce and business. The reality, of course, is that sport and the arts can be competitive to a degree that few in business will ever experience.

When negotiating with the ballet company's manager, the business sponsor is likely to find, not a gifted amateur, but a tough negotiator, who expects and respects hard bargaining as long as this does not interfere with the creative side of his company's programme.

Many of the criteria affecting a sponsorship choice are self-evident, especially for a company that has taken the time and trouble to work out its own particular sponsorship philosophy. How this is done will obviously differ from company to company. However, the first step in taking one's sponsorship activity seriously is to appoint someone of authority within the management team to run the programme even if, in cash terms, sponsorship expenditure may be less than 10 per cent of the advertising or promotional budget. It is just as wrong to try to quantify sponsorship by how much you spend on it as it is to expect a junior executive in the public relations or advertising departments to have the experience and nous to run it for you. In some ways sponsorship is the most visible expression of a company's philosophy. It provides a glimpse of the *soul* of business, an opportunity to correct the unfavourable impression that always seems to have existed.

Charles Dickens' portrait of Josiah Bounderby, the archetypal banker and millowner in *Hard Times*, has haunted board rooms since 1854:

A big, loud man, with a stare, and a metallic laugh. A man made out of a coarse material, which seemed to have been stretched to make so much of him. A man with a great puffed head and forehead, swelled veins in his temples, and such a strained skin to his face that it seemed to hold his eyes open, and lift his eyebrows up. A man with a pervading appearance on him of being inflated like a balloon, and ready to start. A man who could never sufficiently vaunt himself a self-made man. A man who was always proclaiming, through that brassy speaking-trumpet of a voice of his, his old ignorance and his old poverty. A man who was the Bully of humility.

That, added to Shakespeare's Shylock, left writers like Zola, Upton Sinclair and Waugh with only the skeleton of a reputation to pick over.

How do the banks use sponsorship to shake off the 'Bounderby' image? Most of them have well-established charity budgets for responding to appeals and one finds, when talking to the larger banking houses in the City, that even in 1988 the distinction between charity, sponsorship and other activities is by no means clear. National Westminster, for instance, is a member of The Per Cent Club which sets companies a standard, based on a percentage (minimum 0.5 per cent) of profits or dividends, for their total contribution to the community through charitable giving, sponsorship and secondments.

NatWest had no difficulty in meeting this requirement and the relevant slice of their profits in 1988 amounted to around £11 million, about 1 per cent. Ian Griffiths, public affairs senior executive, told me that the lion's share (60 per cent) would go to community welfare efforts to help deprived people, inner cities, etc. A wide range of projects involve the secondment for up to two years of managers either in mid-career or nearing retirement. 'While we seek as high a profile as possible', explained Griffiths, 'We are more concerned with corporate identity – being linked to worthwhile ventures.'

The remaining 40 per cent of this expenditure was divided between sponsorship of the arts and sport with the emphasis on grass-roots participation involving as many people as possible and away from elitist events.'A women's hockey match in Ebbw Vale would probably get preference over, say, showjumping in the Home Counties.'

Not everyone would share this perception of showjumping but the interesting point about the NatWest approach was that the impressive figure of £11 million excluded what most would regard as the bank's chief sponsorship, the NatWest cricket competition. This was allocated a further £2 million over five years but out of marketing funds.

Some companies put sponsorship within their public affairs departments, others create special units to run it, but the efficiency of the operation will depend largely upon the seniority and enthusiasm of the people in charge. They, ideally, should have direct access to their chief executives and/or their boards of directors.

Reporting directly to the board has several advantages, not least being able to reach decisions more quickly over how much money is to be spent. Long-term planning becomes easier because it can be dovetailed into other corporate strategies at an earlier stage. This is important since the benefits of sponsorship are long-term and, if future business plans involve reaching a younger age group, it makes sense to let the sponsorship director know so that he doesn't encumber himself with commitments in the over-50s age group. Incidentally, the old jibe about banks choosing sponsorships on the basis of the chairman's wife's hobbies has another side. Lloyds' Sir Jeremy Morse is a chess lover and this led to a major sponsorship of school chess, which fitted the bank's marketing strategy, and administrators of school competitions certainly found the sudden availability of management expertise to be no burden.

Lloyds also brackets sponsorship with donations, secondment, inner city regeneration and other activities in its overall community strategy. In 1988 it has spent £1.25 million worldwide on sponsorship (£1 million in the UK) and Chairman Sir Jeremy Morse described the policy as being 'focused on supporting the arts, education and design, linking sponsorship to the training and practical encouragement of young people'.

Banks and other institutions obviously need to be concerned with more than money and Morse summed it up this way: 'We can only achieve our aims in the context of a healthy economy and society. So we recognise our involvement and responsibility as corporate citizens in the communities where we work.'

Sometimes, indeed, choosing and running a sponsorship programme may fall to the marketing strategist, in which case it will tend to be more commercially flavoured with measurable returns, such as increased sales, being sought. Sponsorships that are designed chiefly as part of a public relations exercise tend to be less expensive and concerned with improving company image and public awareness. In my case the long-term planning of arts sponsorship for Commercial Union started relatively informally during discussions with the then Chairman, Sir Francis Sandilands who was also Chairman of the Royal Opera House Trust. A sympathetic and enlightened chairman and board of directors obviously are essential to any rational approach to sponsorship.

Music was an obvious first choice for a multinational insurance company because it speaks an international language and because it provides an overlap of potential audiences. Thanks to Sir Francis Sandiland's close association, an early link was established with Covent Garden. CU's first true sponsorship, in the sense of receiving something in return for financial assistance, was with the London Philharmonic Orchestra. This continuing relationship stemmed from a lunch meeting with an old friend, Bill Kallaway, whose consultancy was then acting for the Orchestra as advisers on publicity.

Subsequent CU sponsorships, their management and expectations, were modelled on this association. The Royal Opera House's *Ring Cycle* and other prestigious Covent Garden events, the Europalia arts exhibition in Brussels, and the LPO's 1976 Bicentennial tour to the United States, rapidly put CU among the leading arts sponsors in Britain.

Probably the most rewarding from every point of view was our co-sponsorship of the Schools Prom, the annual November concert at London's Royal Albert Hall, which is filmed by BBC Television and reaches an audience of millions over the Christmas holidays.

This was launched by Times Newspapers Limited in 1975, and Humphrey Metzgen, a *Times* marketing man, had the task of enlisting other commercial support. One day in 1976 he asked me if CU would agree to become a Friend of the Schools Prom (that is, one of several companies paying as little as £100 for the privilege of a box to entertain business associates at the three performances held each year in November). I declined but said we would be interested in joining *The Times* as an equal sponsor, guaranteeing up to £15,000. In 1977 this was to become something of a boon for Derek Jewell, the ebullient Schools Prom Director, whose employers, Thompsons, were soon to enter the long-drawn-out struggle to keep *The Times* going in the face of industrial strife. Derek, as Publishing Director, was heavily involved in these negotiations, but his enthusiasm for the Schools Prom remained undimmed until his death in 1986.

Sadly, all efforts at a solution to the newspaper dispute eventually proved unavailing and our arrival at least provided an assurance that the Schools Prom would survive. As it happened, when in 1981 Thompsons sold *The Times* to Rupert Murdoch, the latter agreed to remain a co-sponsor and, although Derek Jewell joined the mass exodus of managerial talent from *The Times*, he was able to remain for a time as Director of the Schools Prom.

The Schools Prom is a celebration of music at schools and demonstrates the remarkable developments made in teaching music at British schools since 1960. A typical concert will include full youth orchestras, chamber music ensembles, a flute and harp quartet, a brass band, a jazz group, bell-ringers, a West Indian steel band and a group of six-year-olds playing recorders, and the central area is packed with youngsters standing, clapping, cheering in typical Proms fashion whenever the opportunity presents itself.

Famous names, such as John Dankworth, Julian Lloyd Webber, Yehudi Menuhin, Johnny Morris, Ronny Scott, Don Lusher and Terence Judd, have appeared on the programme, and each year we had a group of young musicians from overseas. To see a platoon of Russians launching enthusiastically into 'Land of Hope and Glory', the traditional finale, was a minor bonus. The youngsters themselves thoroughly enjoyed and benefited from this once-in-a-lifetime experience.

Because of *The Times'* problems – its publication was suspended for almost a year – we took over the production of the Schools Prom programme, always a useful exercise for sponsors providing they have the editorial resources. And, remarkably, we improved on *The Times'* performance, turning a £3,000 loss on the programme into a small profit, although reducing the price by 10p and increasing the print run. Friends in Fleet Street observed, somewhat maliciously, that the editorial content, design and style were also an improvement!

While the Schools Prom captures the limelight and the publicity, Derek Jewell was the first to admit that it depended for its talent on the National Festival of Music for Youth which CU also co-sponsors. This is a well-established event, run by Larry Westland, that taps the musical talents of youngsters in 38,000 schools all over Britain. During the year it progresses through local area and regional concerts embracing all kinds of music and musical ensembles to a national concert at the Royal Festival Hall in summer. From this national final a representative selection of the best groups is made to form three evening concerts which are the Schools Prom, and its success is entirely due to the talents of the children and their teachers. The directors and sponsors of the Schools Prom are there to help make this talent known to a wider audience.

Co-sponsorship, of course, is not an ideal arrangement because inevitably there are conflicts of interest, but with an event that is run chiefly for the benefit of children, even the hard-nosed marketing entrepreneur is likely to submerge his demands in the general interest. And so it proved with the Schools Prom. It was fortunate to have two able organisers in Larry Westland, producer, and Derek Jewell. While at times they disagreed totally, the Schools Prom thrived on this blend of contrasting personalities – Jewell's showmanship combined with Westland's command of production. Sharing planning meetings with them was often educational.

There are excellent reasons for linking large companies with the best; the association with excellence, like with like, is attractive. Such élitism can also invite criticism because it is natural that those who criticise business for not coming to the aid of national institutions like Covent Garden will also be the first to complain that such assistance is more necessary lower down the artistic ladder.

At one seminar in London I finished a talk about our sponsorship programme and invited questions from the audience. One came from a well-known correspondent. Having, disarmingly, complimented CU on its enlightened attitude, he asked 'But don't you think you should be spending more at grass-roots level or even devoting this money to curing cancer?'

As it happened, Commercial Union, like most City institutions, has always contributed generously to charity, including medical research, and this is regarded as patronage for which no publicity is sought or considered desirable. It is generally enough to remind critics of this fact.

Another factor to consider is the risk of becoming too closely identified with London. Although CU is a City-based organisation, it has offices worldwide and its United Kingdom division has branches in most British provincial centres. It therefore was sympathetically disposed towards organisations like the LPO and Sadler's Wells when they were planning provincial tours. One of the best exercises in internal staff relations was to sponsor a Scottish Opera production of *Rigoletto* in Glasgow, when the dress rehearsal was given as a free preview for 800 Commercial Union staff and relatives.

With music and youth as the two pillars of CU's sponsorship, it was logical that our return to sport should be at more junior levels: hence the launching of the first Junior World Cup for under-18 golfers, underwriting the under-16 county cricket championships, the boys' and girls' national lawn tennis championships, the under-15 boys' golf championship and so on.

Of these, the Commercial Union Junior World Cup presented the biggest challenge. It is one thing to sponsor an established championship that is run by a sports association or national body; it is quite another to start something completely new, win the co-operation of the sports authorities and then organise and run it and get it accepted by the media and the sports world as a bona fide international event in its own right.

The Junior World Cup idea was hatched over lunch in the Captain's Room at Lloyd's, an appropriate enough venue, since the host was Ted Dexter, the former England cricket captain, who had been putting various sponsorship proposals to me. I explained that we were no longer interested in sponsoring professional sport, but would be interested in doing something for youngsters in golf, which is the traditional insurance game, and preferably something with an international appeal. A team match-play tournament was the outcome of our discussion, and subsequent meetings with Ted and his associate, Rayner Blanch, laid the foundations. This was in October 1979.

We aimed to stage the first event at St Andrews, Scotland, in the following September and much spadework had to be done. It was essential to win the support and approval of the amateur golfing authorities, whose attitude towards sponsorship is understandably cautious. Keith Mackenzie, Secretary of The Royal and Ancient, was sympathetic, and the R and A agreed to help draw up the rules and, if required, provide referees.

Ted and I flew to Paris to enlist the support of the European Golf Federation. The two Frenchmen, Claude Cartier, President, and J. L. Dupont, Secretary, could not have been more helpful and they agreed that their own European championship should be a qualifying event for the World Cup.

The Americans were less co-operative. In Atlanta, Georgia, we faced an indifferent United States Golf Association, who felt unable to select a United States team to compete. However, their Chairman of Junior Golf, Jim Gabrielsen suggested that we approach Mike Bentley of the American Junior Golf Association (AJGA). Gabrielsen, incidentally, told me one of the saddest golf stories. In the final of the British amateur he was all square at the last hole but was just short of the green in two, while his opponent was in a bunker for four. In a nightmare few minutes that he will never forget Gabrielsen took five more shots and lost the hole and the championship with a seven to his opponent's six.

Mike Bentley proved energetic and enthusiastic. Not only that, but the AJGA selected a team that played probably the best golf by under-18s that has been seen on the Old Course. They eventually won the World Cup, defeating England in the final (Paul Way, one of the England pair, went on to win the English amateur championship the following spring and subsequently play in the British Walker Cup team before becoming a professional and a Ryder Cup star as well).

With 16 countries taking part, the preparation, travel arrangements, accommodation, administration, entertaining, looking after the press and television and the hundred and one other unsuspected golf tournament items, made sponsoring such an event a demanding exercise, quite apart from managing the competition itself.

We chose St Andrews for the first World Cup because it is the home of golf but, being a public course, it is not the easiest venue at which to stage a championship. We block-booked teeing-off times months ahead to avoid colliding with casual golfers but we could not use any of the R and A Clubhouse facilities. Instead, we set up our admin. centre in Rusack's Hotel, overlooking the eighteenth green, just down the road from the St Andrews Club, and this solved our changing-room and dining problems. The team's living quarters were about two miles away in St Andrews University.

The Ladies Golf Union van was hired for use as a mobile starter's office, since we had to use both the Old and New Courses and from the R and A we rented some walkie-talkie equipment that proved temperamental. The wind blew cold from the east, causing the Singapore boys to put on two or three sweaters. The Japanese complained about the lack of telephone communications to Tokyo. The Americans were critical of the league format but subsequently agreed that it worked well and was the fairest method: we had four leagues of four teams who played each other over the first three days, two singles and a foursome; league winners then went on to a knock-out semi-final to produce the finalists.

But by the end of the week all the team managers voted the Junior World Cup a major success and it became evident that it should be an annual fixture. Perhaps the most significant endorsement was an approach shortly after from the Professional Golfers' Association asking if they could become associated with the Junior World Cup.

In 1981 the Junior World Cup was retained by the United States, again beating England in the final at Portmarnock, near Dublin, in some of the toughest conditions of wind and rain that locals could remember. The following year Spain defeated England to take the trophy in Atlanta, Georgia, on Bobby Jones's old course, the Atlanta Athletic Club.

Spain included an up-and-coming youngster called Olazabel – who also went on to Ryder Cup fame – but England's consolation was a semi-final victory over the United States, the first defeat suffered by an American team on their own soil. Many other Junior World Cup youngsters went on to achieve golfing prominence, including England's David Gilford and Mike McLean, and Sam Randolph jr and Billy Andrade of the United States.

When I reported to the Board of Directors each January I reviewed the previous year's activities and outlined plans for the forthcoming year. Invariably, the questions that followed revealed a growing curiosity about sponsorship and its usefulness. The first of such annual presentations set out the basic precepts upon which the company's philosophy of arts sponsorship was based. These were as follows:

(1) Sponsoring the arts is a responsibility that business should be prepared to assume as part of its role in society.

(2) Using such sponsorship as a means of publicising the company is entirely acceptable if done with restraint and good taste.

(3) Arts sponsorship can, in addition, yield other benefits apart from improving the sponsor's public image by means of appropriate publicity.

(4) It provides opportunities for good staff relations, contributes to the welfare of society by enlarging artistic horizons and enabling arts organisations to reach wider audiences and so improve the quality of life.

(5) Since it is clearly impractical to respond to all the hundreds of requests for assistance received, it is sensible to confine our major arts sponsorship within a particular area.

(6) In this way one achieves a long-term association that, by its implied guarantee of help, reduces financial anxiety for the sponsored organisation, leaving it free to concentrate on the artistic and creative function.

(7) The efficient managing of a sponsorship programme depends upon good personal relationships with the sponsored organisation. Deciding to send a cheque is the beginning, not the end of involvement.

(8) It is important for staff at all levels to be involved with a company's sponsorship.

As we have seen, there are several methods of sponsorship and a company may use more than one. Some observers conclude that the ways in which companies select activities to sponsor and the people they make responsible for sponsorship, as well as the extent of their involvement, indicate which are serious sponsors and which regard sponsorship as a cosmetic. Unless one takes sponsorship seriously it becomes a pointless exercise. The 'amateur' and 'professional' approaches are illustrated at one extreme by the casual involvement following, perhaps, a chance remark to a director who happens to have a personal interest in the sponsored activity and, at the other extreme, by the company with a clear profile on sponsorship, a well-defined purpose and the administrative experience to make it work.

Much money can be wasted on ill-chosen or inefficiently run sponsorships. This form of 'dabbling' is irresponsible to staff, shareholders, customers and, indeed, also to those being sponsored. While little harm comes from sending a prize cheque to the local pony club gymkhana in which the company secretary's daughter happens to be competing, it is ill-advised to allow such a casual link to lead to a costly involvement that may be inappropriate to the company's image and objectives. As the Economist Intelligence Unit points out, 'If neither the company nor the sport concerned is properly organised to handle the arrangement, not only will the company waste a considerable amount of money, but resentment may be caused among shareholders, employees and potential customers.' John Wheatley, Director-General of the Sports Council, put it to me this way: 'It's a contract between consenting adults – but they should know what they're consenting to'.

Even a short-term commitment should be whole-hearted. It will be selected to support short-term aims, such as launching a new product, when results are required quickly. Image-building among identified target audiences requires long-term commitments.

A common and quite straightforward method is to put up the prize money for an existing event or competition or to finance a future event in the sponsored activity. It requires more effort to sponsor something new and contribute expertise and management time as well as cash. Few companies like to undertake capital projects, but when they do these can be vitally important. Some soccer clubs have had help in land purchase, or with ground improvements, such as new grandstands. Several named companies are associated in this way with things like the National Equestrian Centre, sports centres and the Crown Green bowling stadium at Blackpool.

A view, shared by many people running sponsorship campaigns for other companies, is that it is more rewarding to have a long-term association. One-off events, such as horse races, can give some value if bolstered by effective publicity, but establishing in the public mind a special link with a sponsored event cannot be done overnight.

When planning an international tournament or championship, both sides should consider at least a three-year arrangement, with the sponsor having an option to renew. One-year commitments are of dubious benefit to either party and a sudden cessation can attract unwelcome publicity. Green Shield's famous Grass-Roots Tennis sponsorship for youngsters, for example, ran for seven years up to 1977 and represented a £1 million investment. It was apparently a totally altruistic effort described as 'excellent' by a Sports Council spokesman. Then came inflation and the oil crisis. Exit Green Shield, leaving behind a bad impression and adverse publicity that seemed unfair in view of their previous contribution.

It is instructive to analyse Green Shield's reasons for deciding to take up sponsorship in the first place. They certainly had no need to advertise their stamps through sponsorship because existing advertising was effective and something like market saturation had been achieved through garages and other outlets, such as Tesco. Their problem was one of image. Trading stamps were not quite acceptable, not really British. 'We wanted to strengthen the image of Green Shield to Mum, to reassure her that we were a stable part of the community, and involved in it,' said a spokesman. 'We weren't trying to sell the product, our ads were doing that very successfully, so we didn't need TV. We just wanted to give ourselves a better image.' They could point with pride to the many thousands of public park players who were introduced to tennis by Green Shield, not to mention national names such as Buster Mottram.

Market researchers reported that the scheme was having the effect intended. Journalists and politicians began to look upon the company image more favourably. The scheme was supported by the Establishment, personified by Prince Philip, and Sir Roger Bannister, then Chairman of the Sports Council. By refusing to allow the sale of goods at Grass-Roots Tennis training events, Green Shield reinforced this respectable image and avoided the suspicion that the event was being used to sell to the youngsters.

When economic reasons led to Green Shield ending the sponsorship they were moving into Argos shops as their main area of operations 'where this scheme was not appropriate.' Perhaps not everyone would agree with the logic of that argument, but it sounds a warning note to sports organisers: when seeking commercial aid they can be vulnerable to market forces outside their control. Said John Carson, Schweppes Marketing Director, 'If we decide that a particular event or programme is not working for us it will receive rather short shrift' (*Campaign*, 13 July 1979).

Businessmen must always be able to respond quickly to market changes and the variety of uses of sponsorship makes it an appealingly flexible medium. It can serve many different aims if it is chosen carefully and managed properly. A half-hearted or amateur approach is no longer acceptable now that sponsorship can cost many thousands of pounds, and Midland Bank is one group which claims that sponsorship needs to be scientifically organised.

Midland Bank first establishes whether it is to be sole sponsor or co-sponsor, and usually declines the latter role. It asks how its money is to be used (e.g. whether to make good a deficit or meet the total bill). It negotiates implacably for free advertising space in programmes and posters, and proposes a bank official to take the spotlight at any prize-giving ceremony. To men in the banking business, writing polite rejection letters to the flood of sponsorship requests is no problem but, like the National Westminster, the Midland Bank keeps a file of 'possibles', which occasionally lead to something worthwhile.

Among such possibles will almost certainly be a representative of educational sponsorships, school projects, student scholarships, and sponsored scholarships for such things as sailing or outdoor training for company employees. This last may be seen as an opportunity for personal development or a means of staff recruitment.

Sport and the arts are the more obvious choices, but many other activities can provide successful sponsorships. We have seen how *Wisden* set the example of sponsored books more than a hundred years ago, an example emulated brilliantly by the *Guinness Book of Records*. The Imperial Group and the Society of Authors have sponsored the British Radio Awards, Watney Mann (not inaptly) the Pub Entertainers Award and the *Daily Telegraph* is associated with the annual ABSA awards to business sponsors of the arts.

A recent and unusual success story was Barclays Bank International's £150,000 sponsorship of the 1975 Everest expedition. This proved a sound investment that yielded, in the end, a profit of £7,000 from such spin-offs as a film, a book, a lecture tour and souvenirs. The public relations value was in the film of the expedition which put Barclays in front of school audiences all around the world.

What about all the other leisure and artistic activities that could provide worthwhile sponsorships? A few years ago darts or snooker might not have seemed attractive, but look what television mileage they have achieved by them. Even dominoes is now considered to have ratings potential. Years ago, as a young sports journalist in Fleet

Street, I asked Kingsley Wright, the *Daily Telegraph*'s Sports Editor, to nominate a minor sport that had the greatest publicity potential.

After a moment's thought he selected bowls, but even Kingsley could not have predicted the immense audiences who would one day be watching the exploits of stars like David Bryant. (Some years later I put a similar question to Kingsley's successor, Radford Barrett, whose unhesitating choice was – volleyball.) But if bowls can appeal, what about croquet? At that time Rugby Union had advanced only a few steps down the sponsorship road. In about 1962 a large tobacco group asked me to suggest a format for Rugby Union sponsorship and I suggested a World Cup for Rugby Sevens. Imagine the television appeal of swift, attacking rugby, in short sharp bursts, with a diverse array of talent from Fijians and Japanese to Americans, Argentinians, Kiwis and Welshmen, all in a concentrated week's tournament at Wembley. It hasn't happened yet, but it will.

Critics of the idea quoted the negative aspects – the South African problem, for example. But they have been proved wrong by such events as the launching in 1987 of a full 15-a-side Rugby Union World Cup which was hailed as an instant success. Wrote John Mason in the *Daily Telegraph*: 'The voyage through previously uncharted water is over. The dreaded unknown of Rugby Union's first world cup, its threat to the ideals and attitudes of conservative administrators among the home unions, has proved harmless in reality.'

The 1980 Economist Intelligence Unit Report predicted that annual sponsorship expenditure in Britain would pass £75 million by 1983 unless there were further serious restrictions placed on tobacco and drink companies. No such restrictions were imposed, but rising costs meant a harder battle to secure sponsorships that would stand out in the public mind. Funding a distinctive type of sponsorship has always been a factor and the Report notes that a new form of sponsorship has started to emerge – on community services. This is scarcely new if one takes into consideration the kind of management secondment schemes carried out by bodies such as the National Westminster, or the social action programmes adopted by companies like General Motors. An enormous and largely untapped field of sponsorship awaits the socially responsible companies. Crumbling community relations, highlighted by riots in Brixton and elsewhere, offer a challenging, not to say daunting, opportunity. Providing sports facilities will not solve deep social problems, but it will help to relieve the boredom and frustration of unemployed youngsters.

And why not women's interests for a change? At one London seminar a professional marketing executive waxed enthusiastic about

Characteristic of potential sponsorship	A Score out of 10 pts	B Weighting	C Total
Natural link with sponsor's product or service		× 3	30
Aptness to corporate image		× 2	20
Identification of audience with sponsor's selected targets		× 3	30
Chairman's personal interest		× 1	10
Geographical links with sponsor's business		× 2	20
Benefit to sponsor's current community relations activities		× 1	10
Benefit to sponsor's staff relations		× 3	30
Aptness to sponsor's previous record in sponsorship		× 2	20
Potential advertising exposure		× 1	10
Potential press coverage		× 3	30
Potential television coverage		× 4	40

Total score (out of 250)

Fig. 8.1 Choosing a sponsorship

Cost and value in sponsorship are not necessarily related. Sponsorship success depends upon planning, effort and imagination. The chart above gives a rough guide to assessing the potential value of a sponsorship project. Give each sponsorship characteristic a points valuation (out of 10) in the light of your own company's requirements. This score goes in column A. Multiply this score by the weighting figure in column B to obtain the possible score for each, and enter it in column C, which gives the possible maximum. At the foot of column C add up the total score out of 250.

painting, clothes designing, holidays, story-writing, and films or video-discs for home or private showing. 'How about dogs or other pets?' he asked. 'How about the zoo or the circus, if your product appeals to children or the family? Is there an opportunity here?'

The way the professional marketing man will answer these

questions will be through *research*. Know your target audience, understand their interests, and then identify and build a sponsorship that will appeal to them. Research will not answer all the questions, but it should help. Figure 8.1 is an introductory guide for those faced with the choice of which activity to sponsor.

A particularly fruitful area in the 1980s for sponsors seeking something different has been environmental conservation and the launch of the Conservation Foundation in 1982 was sponsored by Pitney Bowes, the mailing and paper handling company, following their successful sponsorship of the 'Elms across Europe' project. This tree planting scheme using disease resistant elms was started in 1979 and continues to yield beneficial publicity, introducing the company to a wide section of the community, particularly schools. One liked the notion of using elms propagated in the company's car park in Harlow.

The Foundation soon found other socially-responsible companies willing to sponsor its projects, among them Ford and Trust House Forte, whose Community Chest scheme aimed at improving the local environment all over the country is an example of one of the Foundation's bespoke sponsorship schemes. Few ready-made environmental projects 'taken off the shelf' suit a sponsor's requirements and the possible field for environmental help is bewilderingly varied, ranging from museums, churches and historic homes to nature reserves and expeditions.

The Foundation's policy, based on experience, is to sit down and discover exactly what the sponsor requires and then create a project for it. Its interest covers everything from butterflies to belfries and recent contrasting examples include an award scheme for listed country houses, sponsored by the *Sunday Times* and Jackson-Stops & Staff, and the Bisto Kids' Wonderful World of Nature, which has provided schools with annual projects designed to encourage youngsters to investigate their surroundings.

The Foundation's claim is that, whatever a company's needs – corporate, staff relations, product support, public relations, government relations, local, national or international publicity – it can produce a sponsorship package to fill the bill. It's a proud boast and sceptics may doubt whether the benefits in this area are at all measurable. Yet a classic example of commercial success based on sponsorship is at Stoneleigh in Warwickshire at an organisation called the Rare Breeds Survival Trust. This was established to preserve the genetic characteristics possessed by rare breeds of British farm animals and one of their highly satisfied sponsors has been Volvo Concessionaires Ltd.

Volvo paid £5,000 to fund the Trust exhibition at rural events like the Game Fair. Apart from having Volvo umbrellas and display material, the Trust's popular stand also becomes, in effect, a Volvo trade stand. Alongside the Gloucester Old Spot pigs or the Shetland Soay sheep are ranged the latest Volvo estates. Alastair Dymond, the Trust's chief executive, told me 'Car show tents can be a bit high-pressure and sometimes people are put off by slick salesmen and carpeted surroundings. They find the juxtaposition of Volvo cars and our animals much more relaxing.' And this softer approach is effective. After a recent Game Fair Volvo sold more than 80 cars from a mailing list of 30,000 visitors who took part in a rare breeds quiz run at the stand, with a Volvo car as first prize. An income of up to £1 million from an outlay of around £15,000 is no bad recommendation for sponsorship.

Inevitably, headlines about sponsorship tend to refer to the bigger spenders, but sponsorship works at different levels for dozens of smaller companies. On the Association for Business Sponsorship of the Arts (ABSA) annual awards list you will find, among names like IBM, British Petroleum or NatWest, an obscure firm of estate agents (James Henry) taking a best first-time sponsor award for supporting the production of David Pownall's *The Viewing* at the Greenwich Theatre. This company, like the firm of solicitors which part-sponsored an evening's performance by Opera North for the benefit of around 50 staff and customers, is at the other end of the scale. Banks, insurance groups, oil and tobacco companies are in the first division of sponsors; they have sponsorship budgets of around £1 million and their headquarters are often located in London.

The smaller, regionally-based companies in the lower leagues, whose sponsorship expenditure is measured in hundreds rather than hundreds of thousands of pounds, are beginning to exert an influence especially in arts sponsorship. These companies have also become involved with local sports clubs and organisations which they have sponsored, at modest cost to themselves, over many years.

Colin Tweedy of ABSA welcomes this trend to supporting local arts and cites the examples of a Leicester bakery that spent its advertising budget at Christmas on sponsoring a children's pantomime, thus no doubt winning the deserved admiration and support of its customers. And often a local initiative, like that of the estate agents referred to above, will receive wide acclaim. Says Colin: 'A small local brewery in Dorset sponsored a community play involving 500 people from the neighbourhood and the play was so successful that the National Theatre put it on in London'. Similarly, the large sponsors are now keener to show a balanced programme and are supporting, albeit in a minor way, contemporary, ethnic and fringe arts productions. An example of this was Shell's sponsorship of an exhibition of contemporary Scottish art at the 1987 Edinburgh Festival.

CHAPTER 9

Servicing a sponsorship

At a time when the money supply is tight, competition for funds in both sport and the arts increases, and more and more skill and thought must be invested in the approach to industry and in the servicing of a sponsorship once this has been arranged. Curiously enough, even in such an economic climate a feeling persists that to be funded by commerce is akin to congress with the Devil. Even some football club managers, happily engaged in overt commercial transactions every week at the turnstiles and in the transfer market, feel vaguely uneasy about sponsorship. This attitude was caricatured in an article in the *Guardian*, which expressed horror at the Minister for Art's declaration that industry will have to increase its sponsorship of the arts. The writer, a musician, went on to say that she herself did not bat an eyelid at getting an industrial sponsor, provided that he gave her a blank cheque, got no public credit and did not turn up at the concert. In a perfect world no doubt such paragons exist, but reality requires a different approach.

While it is presumptuous to attempt to lay down rules on how to get and keep sponsorship because, as we now know, every case differs, there are basic lessons which can be learned, and identifying them will save time and disappointment.

First comes the initial approach to a potential sponsor. Like the courting ritual of the animal world, it takes a variety of forms, but the odds against success are appreciably higher. Having done all the necessary research and preparation to make sure that what one is offering will be attractive and relevant to a company's business style, marketing philosophy, corporate profile and so on, it would be sad indeed to waste this effort with a ham-fisted overture.

Anyone who has done that much homework is surely unlikely to make the elementary errors – such as addressing themselves to Mr Jack Smith, Chairman of XYZ company, when in fact Mr Smith retired or died the week before or was knighted in the last honours list. Unlikely? Perhaps, but not an impossibility.

Proposals can be conveyed by simple, hand-written letters or handsome, stiff-covered documents tied up in silk ribbon. The hand-written approach has a personal warmth but may arouse doubts in some minds about the applicant's being professional enough to deliver the goods. The lavish brochure might allay this particular fear but raise the question of whether he is likely to overspend on non-essentials. (It is educational for a sponsor to look back-stage at an opera workshop and wardrobe departments and to see what time and money are lavished on minutiae scarcely discernible beyond the orchestra pit.)

Would a personal visit be wiser? Or a telephone approach? The sheer volume of sponsorship appeals these days makes it impossible for a businessman to see everyone, ideal as that might be. Such interviews would soon become a full-time occupation, leaving no time for the other activities (apart from sponsorship) covered by a corporate affairs or public relations director.

Nor does the telephone approach commend itself. It is irritating to have one's line monopolised by strangers putting over what is, after all, a sales pitch. One particular agency executive, acting for a variety of charities and organisations seeking sponsorship, had the habit of ringing in almost every week with some new offer. All the conversations, each one shorter than its predecessor, ended 'Well, put something in the post if you insist and we'll look at it.'

We both knew that he was simply going through the motions and shopping around and, (who knows?) by sheer persistence, may have worn enough people down to claim a sort of success. But was he really tailoring product to customer? He seemed to me to be the worst kind of advocate for sponsorship, and probably responsible, in the long run, for switching off more interest than he generated. If you request over the phone a ten-minute chat and then turn up with two assistants, video presentation and so on you will not endear yourself to busy management either.

The late Patric Hutber, formerly Financial Editor of the *Sunday Telegraph*, was adept at charming money from industry and the City. Although his efforts were on behalf of specific charities, some of his ground rules, as explained during an interval at Covent Garden, could apply to sponsorship applications.

Patric always went to individual companies rather than trade associations. He felt he could get a response from an individual chairman much more readily than from an association which he compared to a committee that had 'neither a soul to be saved nor a behind to be kicked'. He insisted that the only way he could get money from people was to write to them personally on his own notepaper, not more than a couple of sheets, ending up with a sentence like 'I have deliberately kept this letter brief, but I shall be happy to provide any additional information, answer any questions and come to see you if you wish'.

He felt that the generalised appeal, especially in the City, was a waste of time. Circulars were all much the same, but a personal letter could convey a real sense of conviction if written with passion. Always his appeal was accepted or turned down on the basis of his letter.

An example of a professional, but not too glossy, presentation that could be a model for putting across an informative, convincing and well-reasoned case is the brochure *Why Sponsor?*, produced some years ago for the Oxford Playhouse Company entirely free by Holbrook Printing Company Limited, Coventry (itself a telling sponsorship acknowledged on the inside cover). Black and white photographs from previous productions hint at the calibre of production through familiar faces of actors such as Tenniel Evans, Richard O'Sullivan, Jane Asher and Frances de la Tour. A paragraph explains that the Company (Anvil Productions Limited) is a non-profit distributing company and a registered charity, controlled by an independent board of directors and that, apart from being Oxford's resident repertory, it tours throughout the United Kingdom and in the past two years has visited seven countries in the Far East and South America.

On the facing page is a succinct summary of the advantages of sponsorship, with the obligatory quote from Norman St John-Stevas. Overleaf, alongside further scenes from past productions, is a list of achievements by the company in its six years' life (for example, 'Played for 300 weeks in over 60 theatres throughout Britain – organised regular schools' matinées and workshops for an audience of over 50,000 children – played to a total of nearly three-quarters of a million people').

A further paragraph sums up the financial situation:

Box-office income represents 43% of expenditure
The other 57% is made up as follows:
   49% Arts Council
   4% Local authorities
   2.5% Southern Arts Association
   1.5% Commercial sponsorship.

One page lists the past year's productions, ranging from Shakespeare to Pinter, with Shaw, Ibsen, Gogol, Osborne, Potter, Miller, Brecht and Schnitzler all represented, as well as Rattigan, Farquhar, Joe Orton and Alan Bennett. Another page gives a catalogue of the sponsors' credits available on posters, display advertising, press releases and so on and the potential audience scale. An updated insert gives the season's shopping list of forthcoming productions and sponsorship fees ranging from Alan Ayckbourn's *Time and Time Again* (cost: £9,000 for four weeks in Oxford and a ten-week tour) to Ariane Mnouschkine's *Mephisto* (a fortnight's run in Oxford for £750).

The remainder of the brochure includes more detailed descriptions of the company in words and pictures, and a graceful tribute to previous sponsors. The whole publication is done with style and flair but without fuss, and gives an impression of honest and enthusiastic professionalism. I should be surprised if this were not a fair reflection of the standard of performance both on stage and in looking after a sponsor's interests. There is, after all, a demonstrable analogy in selling a sponsorship, even in the arts, with a straightforward marketing exercise. This is not to deny that, as Henry Moore says, art has nothing to do with profit and it is not the artist's function to make money.

The fact remains that the performing arts and sport at the highest peaks of achievement cannot survive on goodwill and fresh air, and, if they are seeking funds from the private sector or, indeed, from the State, they have to show that they are businesslike. They do have a product, whether it be opera or a tennis match, and the product has to have customers (i.e. sponsors). The capital investment in a product such as Verdi's *Falstaff* may include theatre maintenance, staffing, a Hockney stage design, production by John Cox, and singers such as Renato Capecchi, Teresa Cahill and Nucci Condo. All carry price tags.

Sponsors have to be convinced that the enterprise is viable, since it would be unrealistic to expect sponsorship for an enterprise that was incapable of being implemented and unlikely to produce revenue (from the box-office, etc.) to help cover its running costs.

Ill-prepared appeals are clumsily written, addressed to the wrong person in the company and show that little if any staff work was done on the potential sponsor before the appeal was made. Such appeals will almost certainly not contain the kind of information likely to aid a decision and invariably arrive at a time when sponsorship budgets are already committed.

In fact, the ineptitude and idleness that sometimes characterises these approaches leads businessmen to wonder about the quality of management that lies behind them and whether the financial plight of the arts and sport is due more to inefficiency than inescapable circumstance. This is, no doubt, an unfair inference but one that is often made largely because this all-important task of raising money is sabotaged by a lack of foresight.

It is surprising, for example, how little espionage is carried out *before* an approach is made. Some people regard a quick reconnaissance of *The Kompass Register of British Industry and Commerce*, or *The Times 1,000*, to obtain a list of companies to be sufficient preparation, without attempting to identify the person responsible for sponsorship within a company or making any effort to meet him, by chance, at one of the dozens of seminars or conferences that are now part of the sponsorship scene.

Although personal contact with a chairman or chief executive through a friend or mutual acquaintance is still useful, it is no longer the golden key that it once was. Invariably, this approach will be passed on to the sponsorship director or his equivalent and so that hurdle has to be cleared eventually.

The aim should be to get to know the sponsorship organiser and to understand his company's philosophy. If you do that, you are in a better position to offer sponsorships that complement and enhance an existing programme. He may already sponsor your orchestra for the occasional concert. Offer him a series of concerts with a particular identity: perhaps all at a venue close to his business interests, or celebrating the music of one composer, or introducing new conductors or soloists, or on the same day of the week.

His company may have shown a tentative interest in sport for youngsters. The development opportunities here are enormous, with educational spin-offs such as posters and instruction books. The sponsorship manager should be regarded as an ally and, even if no partnership is achieved at once, the groundwork will be useful when another opportunity occurs that you know is appropriate to his needs. After all, he has a selling job to do inside his office, persuading directors and staff that sponsorship expenditure is justified.

As anyone trying to sell a sponsorship project to Lloyds Bank should know, Lloyds wishes to appeal to young people and it recognises that successful sponsorships need to continue over a long period in order for the Bank's name to become associated with them. Thus, while it may not be interested in a concert, it might well sponsor an orchestra.

Again, although the Bank generally does not go in for sporting events, its black horse logo must make it more receptive to events that have an equestrian flavour. In fact, it has sponsored the horse-breeding championship (giving an entrée to the agricultural world) and has sponsored pony-judging which links it to a young audience. In recent years, it has become involved in helping disabled children to ride, finding suitable horses and ponies and running the Lloyds Bank disabled riders championships.

That famous black horse also occurs in the Royal Philharmonic Black Horse Pops, a new orchestra created, as a result of a deal between the Bank and the RPO, in response to demands that the orchestra provide concerts and recordings of a popular nature. This renaming of the orchestra and consequent heavy branding featuring the black horse is a significant development akin to the deal Bill Kallaway arranged for Royal Insurance in 1987, whereby the company name was incorporated into the internationally recognised logo of the Royal Shakespeare Company. The RSC, performing to audiences totalling one million each year, agreed to an exclusive sponsoring worth £1.1 million over three years.

A knowledge of corporate strategies gives vital clues to relevant sponsorships. Advertising restrictions (as with tobacco companies), tax and other factors may at any time reduce the importance of the home market and switch the marketing emphasis to exports which, in turn, will make the board room take an international view.

A properly organised sponsorship vendor or consultant will have taken a long view to identify the right level of sponsorship for any potential client, whether a costly national or international event, or a local, even club, event with a spin-off in terms of staff and management involvement for a sponsoring company. Nor will he hesitate to advise a sponsor to change his tactics if he feels that to do so is in his long-term interests, even if it means reducing the scale and cost of a sponsorship. No doubt some do work along these lines, but far too many appear to apply to their task all the logic and research of the once-a-year punter putting his pin into the list of Grand National runners.

While a company's sponsorship manager needs to be convinced that an organisation has done its homework and is looking for him and not just his money, he himself is also obliged to keep in touch with developments so that suitable opportunities are not missed. Companies differ greatly in their attitudes to this and, while it is true that few are actively seeking events to sponsor, as competition steps up companies are going to need to be well informed.

Some students of company giving insist that the sponsorship director, like the man responsible for donations to charities, really loves the nice warm feeling he gets from giving money away and, although he may say that being deluged with appeals is a nuisance, you should not believe him. If giving money away is pleasant, not giving it away must be the reverse. Since 99 per cent of his time is spent in refusing requests, that nice warm feeling doesn't happen very often.

Naturally, a sponsor will always feel more confident about a sponsorship venture if he has a close involvement in it and can use his own resources of management and expertise, such as in publicity or printing, to make sure that that side of things is done well. The logical extension is total involvement, which, in a sense, moves us out of sponsorship into promotion. Good examples are the large cultural and educational exhibitions like the El Dorado, Tutankhamun and Pompeii exhibitions and, more recently, such spectacular successes as Lloyds Bank's Age of Chivalry survey of art in Plantagenet England at the Royal Academy. Sometimes these are almost too successful, as anyone jammed inside the Royal Academy on a hot day will testify.

Colin Knowles, a fellow member (and ex-Chairman) of ABSA's Executive Committee, was Imperial Tobacco's Public Affairs Director and the Pompeii Exhibition grew out of a meeting between himself and John Letts, Chairman of National Heritage. Colin felt it should be possible for Imperial, with all its experience and expertise, to market such a major undertaking so as to recover all or most of its investment. Like a few major sponsors, Imperial could put up substantial 'front money' providing there was an acceptable chance of an appropriate return in publicity, revenue, etc. Subsequent discussions identified the treasures from Pompeii as being the available exhibition most likely to meet the brief. They then went to an independent company (which happened to be the two executives who had successfully run the Chinese Exhibition and had set up in business on their own) and commissioned from them a feasibility study.

The outcome of this study encouraged the next step: discussions with London's Royal Academy concerning the availability of the venue and their fuller participation in the event. This was significant because it is doubtful, for example, that the Italian equivalent of the Arts Council would have released their priceless relics to a group of British tobacconists, whereas they were more ready to talk with the Royal Academy. A committee structure was devised to approve plans. These committees represented the interests of all the parties, whilst the actual day-to-day executive organisation was left to the professionals.

The next step was to appoint as exhibition organisers the company who had undertaken the feasibility study, and they worked very closely with Knowles's office, reporting on a day-to-day and sometimes hour-to-hour basis. A number of Knowles's staff were involved virtually full-time with them in the development of the project. Professor John Ward-Perkins, the leading authority on Pompeii, was appointed academic adviser to the project, and this ensured a proper 'scholarly' content, gave academic tone to it and helped cut ice when it came to organising a programme of educational visits.

Negotiations were conducted principally with the Italian Consiglio Superiore at the national level and with the Superintendent of Antiquities in Naples. The Italians are not the easiest people to deal with since, at a diplomatic level, the words 'yes' and 'no' appear to have been deleted from their language, but eventually they agreed to release a large and representative selection of items for the exhibition.

Colin Knowles and one of the organisers met the Director of the Louvre in Paris to negotiate the release of the Boscoreale silver which was in the permanent collection. Interestingly, the Director's principal reservation at that time was over security against terrorists' attacks. Many bombs had been going off in London during 1975/76 and this was, understandably, making the custodians of irreplaceable national treasures cautious about allowing their artefacts to come to London. Partly to overcome such reservations and also to satisfy the insurers, a retired security chief from Scotland Yard was recruited. He in turn recruited hand-picked security/warding staff.

A highly imaginative designer for the exhibition (Alan Irvine) joined the team, as did an agency to work on the advertising campaign.

The exhibition was strongly underpinned by the following special deals:

(1) British Rail agreed to lay on special trains for students from all parts of the country because of the educational value of the exhibition. Special visiting hours were reserved for student parties and package deal prices were negotiated accordingly.

(2) Local museums of archaeology were also given display material and encouraged to organise special parties.

(3) The exhibition was opened by Princess Anne (a royal opening is always helpful) on 20 November 1976, and other companies and organisations were sold, at a premium price, the facility for private parties to visit the exhibition and for having champagne receptions for their clients in the private rooms of the Royal Academy as a seasonal treat. Of course, Imperial Tobacco made extensive use of these entertaining opportunities for its own management and customers.

Much emphasis was laid on the importance of the financial

contribution made from retailing both catalogues and merchandise, and a merchandise sub-committee of experts was set up to advise on the selection of goods for volume sale at relatively high margins. This did, in fact, prove to be an important contribution.

Advertising eventually appeared on local radio, in the national and particularly the London evening and the regional press and on poster sites made available jointly by the *Daily Telegraph* and Imperial Tobacco from their permanent bookings. The saturation achieved on London underground stations was particularly effective.

The partnership with the *Daily Telegraph* provided two major lead stories in the colour magazine including the cover, and articles and reports relating to the exhibition appeared in their editorial columns virtually every day over three months. Much merchandise was sold by mail order through the newspaper's small ads columns.

Colin Knowles made the following comment on the exhibition:

The results proved better than we dared hope for. The exhibition went like a fair from the first day. Over 630,000 people eventually passed through the turnstiles – we had to apply to the Academy for an extension to keep the exhibition open beyond the originally contracted period. The scale of the enterprise proved to be such that other media could not and did not ignore it: it was extensively covered by television, radio and the national press. We reaped a rich reward in publicity terms and not only did we recover our investment but there was a significant excess of income over expenditure, which allowed us to make further useful disbursements to arts projects.

This exhibition story shows what can be achieved by combining imagination, artistic flair and marketing skill. It is also helpful to have a budget of about £0.5 million to 'get the show on the road'. This, in fact yielded a profit in excess of £100,000.

Companies which lack the experience to administer their own sponsorship activities can now call upon a wide range of professional consultants, who have appeared in recent years. Only a handful existed in 1980 but they now muster more than 200, ranging from companies like Alan Pascoe Associates, which has a £6 million turn-over, to one-man agencies offering specialist advice that can be very cost-effective. Details about them can be found in *Hobsons Sponsorship Year Book*, the first sponsorship directory, launched in 1988 (I have to declare an interest here, since I was asked to be consultant editor to the project). The consultants provide many services, from originating new projects and managing them for a client to handling press, radio and television liaison, publicity, design and so on.

One yardstick by which to measure the health of an industry is the success of the publications it generates. *Sponsorship news* was launched in 1982; it gives a monthly commentary on the sponsorship scene and its scope has widened over the years from covering simply sport and the arts to embrace conservation, charity and media sponsorship as well as hospitality and corporate entertainment. The man behind this monthly publication, and its editor since 1982, is Jonathan Gee, whose marketing career included spells with J. Walter Thompson and Unilever before he set up his own agency in 1976. He had always been involved in sponsorship, initiating the Matchbox Toys sponsorship of Team Surtees in the 1970s. He deserves a niche in sponsorship history since he 'helped bring Durex into big-time motor racing' – and that was long before AIDS made condoms a socially acceptable conversation topic.

Since no two sponsors are alike, different consultancies will suit different customers. For example, CSS Promotions Limited will come up with tailor-made sporting events to satisfy individual sponsors and since they also manage and promote such household names as Daley Thompson, Stirling Moss, Barry Sheene, the England Cricket Team and Alan Minter, they are particularly adept at obtaining television exposure. Their team of writers, editors, illustrators, designers and printers will produce everything from press releases to programmes and brochures. Their clients range from Allied Breweries to Zetters Pools and include the Football Association and the Test and County Cricket Board.

Sports sponsorship, not surprisingly, has spawned most such commercial consultancies, but the focus of interest on the arts in recent years has seen a rise in the number of arts sponsorship consultancies. The first such specialist organisation was set up by Bill Kallaway in London in 1972, and when he discussed his plans with me his interest was divided between the arts and equestrian events.

I was glad to see him concentrate on one thing and now Kallaway (Consultants and Management) Limited can fairly claim to have remained in the forefront of the sponsorship movement with a track record that includes the General Accident's Scottish National Orchestra tours and educational programme, the Leeds international pianoforte competition (with Harveys of Bristol), the Segovia international guitar competition (sponsored, appropriately, by the Sherry Producers of Spain) and the Royal Insurance–Royal Shakespeare sponsorship mentioned above.

A prime source of information for would-be sponsors of the arts in Britain is the Association for Business Sponsorship of the

Arts (ABSA), established in 1976 with Luke Rittner as its Director. Luke subsequently went on to become Secretary-General of the Arts Council and Colin Tweedy succeeded him at ABSA. ABSA has helped considerably to change attitudes towards sponsorship, and critics who complain that it does not help them very much are usually arts administrators who forget that ABSA was established by businessmen to look after the interests primarily of business sponsors as well as acting as an evangelist on behalf of sponsorship.

ABSA issues a market-place bulletin to all members, giving, among other things, details of sponsorship opportunities. The association provides a consultancy service, arranges seminars, conferences and behind-the-scenes visits, and produces a range of information pamphlets, such as one on VAT as it affects sponsorship.

ABSA is not a marriage broker and does not compete with commercial consultancies. It is a company limited by charitable status and, in fact, was set up with the help of a government grant. Its American equivalent, the Business Committee for the Arts, is a private organisation set up in 1967.

ABSA's links with the government are unofficial but seem to be growing stronger, helped, no doubt, by Luke Rittner's elevation to the Secretary-Generalship of the Arts Council. ABSA administers the government's Business Sponsorship Incentive Scheme, aimed at helping the arts. Part of this scheme is the government's challenge-funding – matching first-time sponsors pound-for-pound up to a ceiling of £25,000. The success of this scheme speaks for itself. In its first three years it raised £15.7 million for the arts, of which the government contributed £4.7 million to match the £11 million of new sponsorship money.

Since ABSA was formed, two other organisations have been set up to bridge the gap between sponsor and sponsored. In 1985 the Institute of Sports Sponsorship (ISS) was founded by 14 major sponsoring companies to encourage sponsorship of sport, improve understanding of the value of sponsorship, formulate a code of practice and so on. Although ISS was set up some years after ABSA, its General Secretary, Peter Lawson, told me that at least in its concept it pre-dated the arts body. Lawson had sought to set up such an organisation when the idea of ABSA was being discussed, but no one had believed it would be possible to establish a joint sports and arts association. 'Even before then – in 1973 – the Central Council for Physical Recreation, encouraged by the Duke of Edinburgh, established a sports sponsorship committee', Lawson told me.

A year after ISS was finally born, solicitor Stephen Townley, an expert on the law and tax relating to sponsorship, established The Sponsorship Association, the aim of which is 'to encourage the development and promote the business of sponsorship' in the areas of sport, the arts, conservation and leisure.

CHAPTER 10

Conclusion and outlook

It is reasonable to predict that sponsorship will increase significantly, that it will become more professional and that it will develop in different ways. Debates about the rights and wrongs of business sponsorship and its effects on the sponsored activity will continue, but fewer directors and shareholders will object to a proportion of the budget being spent in this way. There have been important changes in attitudes and in the way business and the public see one another. Today's consumers are better informed, more confident and less in awe of those in authority. They tend to question what they read in the newspapers and see on the television screen. The message for advertisers is clear: they must find new ways to communicate with customers. Persuasion techniques will have to be backed up by long-term public relations. This is where sponsorship has an important role to play and why it is increasingly becoming part of company marketing strategy. The advertising agencies themselves have not been slow to exploit its possibilities.

British business, as one newspaper put it, has discovered

the immense value, in public relations terms, of being seen to be good corporate citizens through sponsorship of cultural events and sport. But besides this the financial position of the arts, particularly in the United Kingdom, is in its most perilous position ever with, on the one hand, inflation biting deep into budgets which are hardly lavish to begin with and, on the other hand, the government, in its enthusiasm to cut expenditure, slicing back its subsidy.

In this situation it is hardly surprising that banking with its high interest rates, one of the few industries enjoying big profits, should appear to be a milch cow. There is, of course, no such thing as a soft touch in banking terms, but whether or not banks expand their sponsorship programmes really dramatically must depend on how committed they are to the concept of sponsorship and how clearly they have identified their sponsorship policies with their general business objectives. The banks are big enough to withstand government pressure and their track record, on the whole, is good enough to disarm those who try to bring moral pressures to bear. They have made it clear that the level of their spending in support of the arts will be determined by the forces of competition and not 'government arm-twisting'.

This retort was in response to the widely reported overtures made by Mr Norman St John-Stevas, then Minister for the Arts, who during 1980 had supposedly suggested to the banks that they set up a £500 million fund to finance the arts. In fact, what he did was to discuss with the chairmen of the five London clearing banks the possibility of endowing a Clearing Banks Foundation for the Arts whose income could support artistic events. He denied mentioning a figure and, on the face of it, the idea was appealing, although £500 million was a shade optimistic. However, the proposal was based on the old misconception of modern sponsorship discussed in Chapter 1. If the five banks had not been competitors in a competitive market, they might well have been happy to submerge their individual interests and become joint patrons in a philanthropic enterprise.

Sponsorship is not philanthropy, and it was mildly surprising to find the Minister lacking advisers with the nous to warn him off such a venture. Even in Utopia the practical problems of administering the fund, deciding who would benefit and to what extent, would be well-nigh insoluble and would require an organisation that could not avoid treading on the Arts Council's sensitive bunions.

Nor did the House of Commons discussions that followed display more enlightenment. Members revealed that the fate of the arts was something few of them had taken the trouble to consider. The level of questions ranged from puerile humour from the Left to hobby-horse riding on the Right. A parallel was drawn by a Scottish Labour MP between the level of profits in a company and its degree of support for the arts, and he suggested that the Minister should tell the banks that, if they did not make more money available, they should be prepared to submit themselves to the kind of taxation borne by the oil companies through the Petroleum Revenue Tax.

Shortly afterwards, I had the opportunity of questioning St John-Stevas about his attitude towards sponsorship, and his answers revealed much greater awareness. All the more sad that in January 1981 he lost his Cabinet seat and joint roles as Leader of the House and Minister for the Arts, and the Office of Arts and Libraries, that he had created as a separate entity 18 months before, went back to its grey anonymity alongside Waterloo Station as part of the Department of Education.

Mr St John-Stevas (now elevated to the peerage) was quick to agree with the definition of sponsorship as a mutually advantageous business arrangement where the sponsor is seeking to achieve a defined objective. 'One of the main objectives of my sponsorship campaign', he said, 'has been to explain to business and arts organisations alike that sponsorship is not simply another form of charity; in fact, the arts offer substantial potential to companies to extend their marketing and publicity policies. Those in the arts should equally regard sponsorship as a marketing tool and exploit their own activities to attract business support and so finance new ventures.'

His chief concern was to see sponsorship accepted at all levels of business and the arts, rather than to seek for a short-term burst of activity which is not sustained. Co-operation between business and the arts needed time. St John-Stevas made probably the most effective contribution of any Arts Minister and the rest of the interview is printed below in full.

Although 'quid pro quo' is now becoming accepted as crucial to any sponsorship deal, do you share fears that the balance could become lop-sided in favour of the sponsor?

Answer: I believe there is some apprehension in the arts about the risk of unacceptable demands by sponsors. I do not think it has happened yet and I hope it never will. I think companies sponsoring the arts do so to associate with an image of excellence. Brash exploitation would probably attract adverse publicity that would damage rather than enhance corporate image, and I am quite sure companies are sensitive to this. A business should work in close association with the arts organisation it is sponsoring, so that each can understand the other's objectives and be sensitive to its views.

Do you think that complete identification with a sponsor in name, style and colour of brand publicity, logo, etc., is undesirable?

Answer: This is a matter for the parties concerned. In principle, I have no objection to brand publicity or the linking of a sponsor's name to an event. Ultimately, it is a matter for the sponsor and the arts organisation to agree the extent of publicity surrounding the event. For different reasons both must be sensitive to public taste.

The Arts Council have expressed disquiet at the amount of publicity and acknowledgement obtained by sponsors, especially

compared with that given to the Arts Council. Do you share this concern?

Answer: Yes, the Arts Council does an outstanding job and should always receive full credit for the fact. To date it has chosen to be fairly discreet about the amount of publicity it receives in programmes and on posters and so on.

In the highly competitive London orchestral world do you have a formula that will enable London to continue to possess four first class orchestras which are not plunging deeper into the red?

Answer: I am concerned that the arts should continue to flourish and I am, of course, particularly anxious in the present difficult circumstances. The orchestras receive substantial assistance from the Arts Council through the London Orchestral Concert Board and I hope this funding can be maintained as far as possible, despite cuts in public expenditure.

I also know the orchestras are alert to business sponsorship and have been for many years. I hope they will continue to exploit the opportunities in this field. However, I think marketing will have to play an important part as well. Ticket subscription schemes, direct mail techniques, discounts – all these may be necessary: efficient marketing is going to be very important in the future.

Arts sponsors complain at the ambivalent attitude of newspapers, television and radio over arts and sport. Mention of a sports sponsor is now almost taken for granted. Arts sponsors are usually ignored despite agreements with the BBC. Would you care to comment?

Answer: The media are becoming more aware of the significance of business sponsorship of the arts and there has been a definite increase in credits in recent months. However, I agree that references are still inconsistent and therefore unsatisfactory, and I am concerned lest this should deter potential sponsors. I have been told that the omission of a credit in the press is often for no other reason than rigorous sub-editing. This may be an over-simplification, but certainly the arts critics of the major newspapers are conscious of the need to mention the sponsor in reviews and I am not aware of any editorial policy to delete these references. I hope that this problem will resolve itself in time, but I shall keep it under review. There are also heartening signs that the BBC are now more consistent in their references to sponsors in broadcast concerts.

Do you consider trade union involvement in arts sponsorship desirable?

Answer: Yes I do. When I launched the campaign I invited a distinguished group of people to serve on a committee of honour to advise me on various aspects, and I am very pleased that one of the members is Clive Jenkins, who is a very keen advocate of the arts. I hope that through him we can develop a policy to involve trade unions.

Although there has been a multiplicity of commercial and quasi-official organisations offering or selling sponsorship advice, most successful sponsorships depend upon a direct and lasting relationship between sponsor and sponsored. How would you like to see this encouraged?

Answer: Before I answer your specific question, I should like to acknowledge the work of the marketing consultants who specialise in business sponsorship of the arts. They have been responsible for some highly imaginative and very successful arrangements. I agree that, as a general principle, the most successful sponsorships depend upon a lasting relationship between the sponsor and the sponsored and that close contact is essential at all times. I think the greatest encouragement is the experience of a successful sponsorship arrangement. The Government has already made certain concessions to promote sponsorship by businesses, but the best encouragement is to demonstrate to people through practical experience. As I said earlier, we are not talking about charitable giving or moral responsibility, but discussing marketing policy for business and the arts alike. I think companies must see for themselves what can be done. My campaign has tried to explain to those who may not have considered sponsorship before what can be achieved, and, wherever possible, I have tried to use examples of existing sponsorship successes.

Much heat is generated over the question of changes in tax laws to encourage more sponsorship. Do you feel that perhaps not enough emphasis is placed on the fact that sponsorship expenditure can be regarded as a form of advertising promotion and so qualify for tax exemption in the appropriate way (e.g. 52 per cent for companies paying corporate tax)?

Answer: Since it took office the Government has reduced the minimum qualifying period for covenanted payments to charities from over six years to over three years and introduced tax relief on the higher rates of income tax in respect of covenanted payments by individuals up to an annual ceiling of £3,000. These concessions were designed to ease the position for donations, and the arts benefit considerably as most arts organisations are registered charities. There are signs that they are not widely enough known and used.

You mention the provision under Section 130 of the Incomes and Corporation Taxes Act 1970 whereby revenue expenditure incurred 'wholly and exclusively' for the purposes of a trade can be offset against tax. The Inland Revenue instructed its inspectors to advise companies at the outset whether sponsorship deals would qualify in this way, so there is now every opportunity for companies to frame their proposals so as to get the maximum tax relief. I hope businesses are aware of this concession by the Inland Revenue.

Sponsorship, especially in the theatre, tends to play safe for fairly obvious reasons. To some extent this also applies to the other performing arts with the result that funds tend to go to the familiar, the traditional, the tried and trusted, at the expense of the experimental, the innovative, the adventurous. Do you see a way of encouraging business to be more adventurous (and also arts organisations) and so get closer to the spirit of the times and indeed the spirit of the younger generation?

Answer: I can think of several notable recent examples of sponsorship that have gone to 'adventurous' art forms: an exhibition of *avant garde* British Art at the Royal Academy, a travelling Children's Theatre sponsored (for the second year) by a shoe manufacturer, and numerous examples of writers and artists 'in residence'. Within the 'conventional' art forms a more varied repertoire is also being explored. However, taking an overall view, your statement is a fair representation of the present position. I think we are at the start of something that will grow, and as more businesses become involved I believe their competitive edge will encourage them to explore all the various art forms. I am concerned that sponsorship should be considered at all levels in the regions as well as the capital. I am trying to encourage a favourable climate in which sponsorship can develop. I believe we have been successful so far. Ultimately it is a matter of self-help by the arts who must sharpen their perception of their commercial potential. Equally, the business world must become more aware of the unique opportunities offered by the arts. I believe this co-operation is here to stay.

Fears about the possible inhibiting effects of business sponsorship find an echo in the American experience. For instance, corporate art collections, often breathtaking in their scope and splendour, are regarded by some critics as the Muzak of the visual arts. One commented 'Many of them are pretty and superficial, not necessarily substantial in meaning. Most corporations are not interested in quirky or individualistic art. They are interested in broad appeal and pleasing their corporate environment and image.'

Experience of visiting American corporate headquarters tends to support the impression that most favour large, abstract works or, if representational, works without figures. While this encourages some young artists, it excludes others, imposing a cultural bias in art. I suppose centuries ago one might have levelled a similar criticism at the Vatican for imposing a religious bias on artists.

The quality of corporate collections does not escape criticism. Allan Frumpkin of New York's Frumpkin Gallery has accused corporate programmes of being slick or lacklustre. He is not alone in pointing out that the new market has attracted people out to make a fast dollar in the guise of art consultants.

In Britain, doubtless, such sharks also exist, but corporations lacking confidence in their own knowledge and taste in art do have access to a number of tried and trusted advisers and organisations and Nancy Balfour of the Contemporary Art Society is an example. She has proved a wise and able mentor to many companies, and the Society exists to provide that service, being non-profit-making, and to encourage contemporary young artists.

Some companies take the opportunity of acquiring modern collections when moving into new premises and the Commercial Union's headquarters in the City of London, completed in the late 1960s, once housed a fine collection of works by contemporary artists, including Bacon, Nicholson, Sutherland, Nolan and Hockney. After the retirement in 1983 of Sir Francis Sandilands, the chairman, this collection was reduced – an error of taste and of commercial judgement.

As yet, the British art market has not felt a dramatic impact of this form of sponsorship, which is also a very real investment. The possibilities are unpredictable, as the following incident, referred to by the *International Herald Tribune*, illustrates.

Two wealthy companies were bidding for a painting that they both felt would enhance their 'corporate aesthetic', a piece of corporate jargon now popular in the US business circles.

The painting was not one of the artist's best which were then selling at about $400,000 each. But the rival bidders were keen on this particular work for image and publicity and, because a few hundred thousand dollars did not mean that much in their overall budgets, the painting went for $1 million. Since then works by the artist have increased substantially in price.

These are matters for concern. So too are the complaints against business sponsorship of the performing arts that have been voiced repeatedly. They are neglect of the *avant garde*, the tendency to withdraw from specific ventures after a year or two, and the implication that sponsorship is purely charitable. A business sponsor might well point out that he has other priorities and that the *avant garde* should rightly be promoted by the Arts Council, which exists for that purpose as well as for making the arts more accessible to all.

The criticism about withdrawing support after a year or two might have sounded a shade ironic to the Old Vic, the National Youth Theatre, the Shaw Theatre, the City of London Festival and dozens of other organisations which overnight found themselves without Arts Council aid in the financial blitz announced in December 1980. Not many business sponsors display quite such surgical detachment when applying the financial knife.

Lord Redcliffe-Maud in his 1976 report on the arts, said at the time of writing the arts are in such dire financial straits that all we can hope to do is to secure survival. But, besides that, we can use the survival period to set our house of patronage in such good order that, as inflation comes under control, we can be sure of making progress towards a level of investment in the arts that bears defensible comparison with our potential as a nation of artists.

If anything, those 'dire straits' have worsened, despite the fact that the level of inflation has fallen since 1976 and investment in the arts by business has risen dramatically.

In sport the beneficial effects of sponsorship can more easily be recognised and even the over-exposure of main-line sports, such as tennis and motor racing, could eventually divert much-needed funds to less popular but equally deserving pastimes. There may, indeed, be a case for the Sports Council to look again at its scale of financial aid (detailed in Chapter 3) in the light of known support from sponsors and switch more help to where it is most needed and so avoid the present situation in which the rich seem to get richer and the poor starve.

If business is expected to regard sports sponsorship not only as an effective marketing exercise but as part of its social audit, then sports authorities and sportsmen and women, for their part, must reappraise their role. The greed and unreliability of some sporting stars do long-term harm.

Sponsors who feel they are getting a raw deal will either pull out altogether or demand much greater control. Should they gain this authority, sponsorship will give way to full-scale promotion in which sport is run for the benefit of the promoting company and not primarily for the sake of the sport itself. There are already signs that sponsorship, the once mutually beneficial partnership, may have outlived its usefulness and that the sponsor is becoming the agent that will finally turn sport into just another branch of the entertainment business.

Index